Wheels In Motion

Gerald Perschbacher

Published by

700 E. State Street • Iola, WI 54990-0001

Please call or write for our free catalog of publications. Our toll-free number to place an order or to obtain a free catalog is (800) 258-0929. Please use our regular business telephone (715) 445-2214 for editorial comment and further information.

Library of Congress Catalog Number: 96-76698
ISBN: 0-87341-453-5
Printed in the United States of America

Wheels in Motion

Contents

Introduction and Dedication

> "All signs point to the motor vehicle as the necessary sequence of methods of locomotion already established and approved. The growing needs of our civilization demand it; the public believe in it, and await with lively interest its practical application to the daily business of the world." *The Horseless Age,* Vol. 1, No. 1, November 1895.

A hundred years ago giants in-the-making walked the earth, and we didn't know it. Some were short in form, frail or stern looking, hardly the image of great men. But in them was greatness born of a dream.

"Much of their work is in an unfinished state; many of their theories lack demonstration; but enough has already been achieved to prove absolutely the practicality of the motor vehicle," reported *The Horseless Age* in November 1895. Even then the great ambitions of giants were recognized.

We now look back over a century of accomplishments for the American automobile industry. The men who became giants in the industry are long gone, but many of their hopes and dreams remain. Wheels are in motion everywhere and the wanderlust derived from the freedom of transportation granted by the automobile continues unabated.

Those giants were their own wheels in motion, accomplishing feats never before realized against odds that seemed insurmountable. Some resorted to wheeling and dealing to reach their goals. Some of a quiet bent gave support to others with business acumen to achieve their dreams. But all were important wheels in the operation of history. They, and their cars, were wheels in motion.

Without their drive toward success, the 20th century would not have been what it was.

This book is dedicated to their memory.

Gerald Perschbacher
July 1996

In the late 1940s Charles Duryea claimed that this was the actual car which won America's first race in Chicago, Nov. 28, 1895. (Driver is Charles Duryea.)

Charles B. King, at the tiller of his automobile in 1896, the first car to run successfully on the streets of Detroit. Henry Ford is credited with fielding the second car to run on the city's streets. (Photo by John A. Conde)

In his own handwriting to A. L. Dyke, another pioneer, Charles Duryea noted how this was the car used in its first "pulling test," on April 19, 1892.

Chapter 1

High Point for the Industry

The best of times seemed certain. So with pride the American automobile industry marked its 50th anniversary in 1946. It was a turning point in history. Never again would the industry stand so strong and with so much promise.

The Automotive Golden Jubilee was celebrated in Detroit, which had the honor of putting more automobile wheels in motion than any other city on earth. The jubilee epitomized the advancement of the motorized vehicle but especially centered on the industry that it spawned and that had come of age in its first half century. The industry was necessary, since its vehicles had proven crucial as part of daily life for work, health, public safety, and business. Communities drew closer together through commerce and the improvement of roads, thanks to motorized transport. Families took to roads as if their cars gave them wings, escaping their locales for new vistas. If there was any single invention that shaped the 20th century it was the automobile. And of all nations, the impact was felt most keenly in America.

By 1946 the industry had proved its resiliency. Hundreds of manufacturers had come and gone, yet the automobile and a handful of makers remained, stronger than ever. World War I and especially World War II had given opportunity for the industry to show its worth. For World War II the industry had valued its production of aircraft, military vehicles, tanks, marine equipment, guns and artillery, ammunition, parts, and other items at $28.97 billion. By the time of the Golden Jubilee the industry had become ingrained in the economic advance of the nation. The industry was using more than 18 percent of all steel in the United States, 51 percent of all malleable iron, 68 percent of all leather (for upholstery), 75 percent of all plate glass, and 80 percent of all crude rubber. It employed more than 6.5 million workers directly and indirectly, purchased and processed huge amounts of raw materials and farm products, and shipped more than 3.6 million carloads of freight by train annually. It stimu-

Conde Was There

John A. Conde was only 28 years old when the Automotive Golden Jubilee was held. He was on the public relations staff of Nash-Kelvinator Corp. and became aide to pioneer Charles B. King. King's early automotive achievements in Detroit had made him a local hero in 1946. King had come from Larchmont, N.Y., to be at the jubilee. He was among the more mentally and physically alert pioneers.

The Automotive Golden Jubilee "was a hastily conceived event," Conde recalls. It was the brainchild of George Romney who believed that in light of labor and supplier difficulties in 1946, it would be wise to honor the last pioneers and get some positive international attention for the industry. Involved were all the auto makers in America: GM, Ford, Chrysler, Packard, Hudson, Nash, Studebaker, Willys-Overland, Crosley, Checker, Kaiser-Frazer, and truck makers, too, such as White, Autocar, Diamond T, Federal, International Harvester, Mack, and Peterbilt.

"In a matter of just a few weeks an elaborate plan was put into action at Romney's suggestion," says Conde. There were two basic committees: one had representatives from the auto industry and was headed by William S. Knudsen; the other was a community group headed by Prentiss M. Brown, chairman of Detroit-Edison. Other lesser committees were formed.

Conde calls the event "a huge national success." It carried a special degree of success for Nash, since the selection for queen of the jubilee was Mary Grace Simescu, from Nash's advertising production department! Nash also had Conde write and produce a commemorative booklet with a gold-colored title, "Nash 1902-1946." It was handed out at the event. Packard, Studebaker, Chevrolet, and others also issued special folders to mark the jubilee.

Each auto maker was asked to have cars on display, showing the progress of the automobile. Nash borrowed a 1902 Rambler from the Cameron Peck collection in Chicago, displayed a company owned 1909 Rambler, showed a 1918 model Nash (the first one designed by Nash) and also exhibited a 1923 LaFayette. A new 1946 Nash was on hand. Packard had eight cars, the oldest being its first car of 1899, a company owned 1901 model was on display, and a new Clipper was shown. Studebaker had one of the most interesting displays, Conde notes: an 1824 carriage, an 1865 carriage built for President Lincoln, and a 1947 Studebaker—showing how the maker had grown from carriage builder to car maker in 50 years.

But among Conde's greatest delights at the event was having a freelance photographer capture the image of Henry Ford talking with Charles Nash, while Conde stood a scant 6 feet away!

The photo Conde likes best: Charles Nash, left, talking with a weak and aged Henry Ford at the jubilee. (Photo by John A. Conde)

lated the construction of the greatest highway system in the world which had grown from 88,000 miles of improved roads in 1896 to 1.45 million miles by 1946. Had it not been for the design of the internal combustion engine, which by 1946 was powering every new car in America, perhaps even the airplane would not have left the ground early in the century and with such success.[1]

The Golden Jubilee recognized 1896 as the automotive industry's formative year. In some ways, it was a contrived date but seemed logical. Although there had been experimentation with vehicular development earlier in the 1800s by such men as Stuart Perry in upstate New York, Alfred Drake in New York City, James F. Hill in Pennsylvania, George Brayton in Rhode Island, and Charles H. Black in Indiana, no ongoing mass production took place as a result of their endeavors.

Historians in the 1940s traced the first successful American automobile to Charles E. and J. Frank Duryea. They had based their vehicle on the achievement of the bicycle as a means of transportation.[2] The first successful operation of their car was recorded in the September 22, 1893, edition of the Springfield, Mass., *Evening Union*. In 1896 the Duryea Motor Wagon Company was

The trucking industry was honored almost as an offshoot of the auto industry in 1946. However, some auto makers such as Packard, which had abandoned the truck field, made little note of their trucking history during the 50th anniversary celebration.

begun. More than that, they had cultivated a business from their automobile production, being the first such company in America. In 1895 the Duryea Motor Wagon Company of Springfield, Mass., was formed and 13 Duryeas were built—two of which were shipped to England for the Brighton Emancipation Run of 1896.[3]

That year was marked by other advances in the field. On March 6, 1896, Charles Brady King, who drove one of two finishers in the famous *Chicago Times-Herald* auto race the previous year, introduced Detroit to the modern automobile and foreshadowed the main industry for the city. In 1896 the print industry was turning attention to the motored newcomer as more than a fad. Competitive endurance races had already been held in Chicago and elsewhere the year before and were gaining in fashion for 1896 with races at Narragansett Park, R.I.

"The motor car idea is older than history," wrote Charles E. Duryea in 1909. "Homer tells of it in the 18th century book of *Iliad* that Vulcan in a single day completed 20 wheeled-tripods," which were spirit-moved. In 1909 Duryea stated that the industry

Charles B. King, left, alongside a young John A. Conde at the jubilee celebration. Conde was the aide to King. (Photo by John A. Conde)

In 1946 motordom's Golden Jubilee was celebrated in Detroit with a massive parade involving antique vehicles mainly supplied by collectors and floats by auto makers. New cars were also promoted.

likely began in 1895 but that by 1896 it was a certainty.[4] Detroit felt differently, for good reason. It needed a celebration in 1946.

In 1945 and 1946 stoppages had brought the automotive industry to numerous halts since the conclusion of World War II. Many women wished to stay at their jobs since they had entered the work force while "the boys" fought overseas. Soldiers were returning, necessitating their incorporation into the work force. There were upheavals by labor and quality control problems. Market controls dictated by rationing from Washington, D.C., were being lifted and prices escalated. Money that had been earned during the war years could be spent more freely on items many people had wanted but previously had been restrained from getting. Amid this, labor costs were on the rise, large quantities of certain raw materials were very hard to get, and America was adjusting to its role as a major postwar world power.

Was the Golden Jubilee established to facilitate closer

cooperation of labor and management? Some historians say yes. Was the jubilee meant to gain attention for the American automobile industry as new cars were coming off the line, albeit in relatively small quantities? Definitely yes. Was 1946 selected as the celebration year since the industry did not have the time and energy to put toward the jubilee during the war? Possibly. And there is another reason 1946 was the jubilee year: time was short.

Only a small count of automotive pioneers were alive in 1946, but for some the end was near as former big wheels slowed in their motion. Fourteen living pioneers were honored at the celebration and inducted to the American Automotive Hall of Fame in 1946: Henry Ford who had put the common man on wheels; George M. Holley of carburetor fame, representing suppliers; Alfred P. Sloan, Jr., chairman of General Motors and a pioneering engineer (though he was honored, he did not attend); William C. "Billy" Durant, the visionary behind the formation of GM; Ransom E. Olds, the first mass producer of cars in America; Charles B. King, who introduced Detroit to the automobile; Charles W. Nash, former president of GM and the power behind the company bearing his name; Edgar Apperson, a founder of Haynes-Apperson in Indiana; and J. Frank Duryea. Also included were representatives for related industries: Barney Oldfield, credited as the country's first great automobile racer; Charles S. Snyder, an auto dealer who began selling cars when he was 18 years old; Frank Kwilinski, a native of Poland who had completed 60 years of continuous service with Studebaker; John Van Benschoten, who began selling cars in the late 1890s and represented dealers; and John Zaugg, a Swiss lathe operator who had worked for 51 years with the White Motor Company, a clear nod to a company that had begun making cars but settled into trucks.[5]

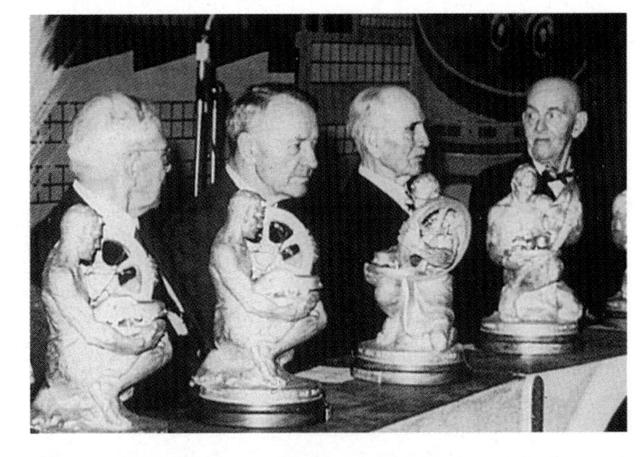

Pioneers who were honored at the jubilee event received special statues in salute of the anniversary. From left are Ransom Olds, Barney Oldfield, Charles Nash, and Charles Snyder. (Photo by John A. Conde)

Henry Ford, left, chats with George Holley during a ceremony at the jubilee. (Photo by John A. Conde)

Of these men, Oldfield was to die less than four months after the jubilee. Ford and Durant would die the next year. Nash would pass in 1948. Olds would go in 1950, King in 1957, Apperson in 1959, Sloan in 1966, and Duryea in 1967. Advanced age, the onset of failing memory, and frail health made it crucial to hold the celebration soon.

Even some organizers were slowed by the years. Lt. Gen. William S. Knudsen, who had organized the industries nationwide for the recent war effort, headed the executive committee for the event. He was tired, in ill health, and would die in 1948. Powell Crosley, Jr., also not a young man, was an afterthought to the committee, coming on about two months before the jubilee.

The Automotive Golden Jubilee was a 12-day celebration held May 29 through June 9. It heightened the importance of

Mercury's 1946 and 1947 offerings were well received by a car-hungry public. But at the time of the jubilee celebration in Detroit, the Mercury was little more than a warmed over pre-war car.

years past and the potential of those yet to come. The American Automobile Manufacturers Association, with George Romney as its general manager, spearheaded the cooperative effort that coordinated many auto-related industries in one grand spectacle.

"A Tribute to the Pioneers" was held at the Masonic Temple with a crowd estimated at about 1,200. Many were industry leaders. The pioneers were honored on stage at a massive table. Each received a special bronze statue. The event was carried on radio. John A. Conde was one of the event participants, assigned as an aide to Charles B. King. King "was to star in almost every activity because he had built and driven the first car on the streets of Detroit in 1896," Conde says. During the events, the 78-year-old King introduced him to Henry Ford. Conde was surprised at Ford's weak handshake, a sign of his frail condition. Each car maker was asked to provide an aide for a pioneer. The treasurer of Nash-Kelvinator was aide to Mr. Nash, and Henry Ford II was aide to his grandfather.[6]

It was a bold stroke to bring the might of automotive Detroit to the minds of Americans in 1946. Many new car buyers were becoming disenchanted while waiting for cars. In July 1946 it was reported that passenger car production was 1,666,000 below

DeSoto fared about the same as Ford and Mercury in bringing out its old style amid the hoopla of the 50th anniversary for the auto industry.

The Buick float in the anniversary parade down Woodward and East Jefferson Ave. made use of the bombsight hood ornament that had become the make's styling symbol.

expectation. This came to a loss of $1.5 billion. The industry had hoped to drive 2,320,000 cars off their lines for the first six months of 1946. Actually, only 654,000 were made. The rate of 500,000 per month for the entire industry was expected by the time of the Golden Jubilee. But for June only about 140,000 units were reported. Even newcomer Kaiser-Frazer, which was shrewd in obtaining raw materials for production, had to delay its initial shipment of Kaiser Specials and Frazers until June 22, 1946. That first shipment of 1947 models went to the Muntz Car Company, Los Angeles distributor, a concession to Henry J. Kaiser's industrial West Coast influence.[7]

Milestones were noted during the time of the jubilee. Very active in the jubilee was Nash Motors. In ads, the company took its history back farther. It explained that its tradition of body building went back 100 years to 1846 "when the seed of the great Seaman enterprise was planted" in the vehicle body building business. Seaman built its first automobile bodies in

James Melton, nationally known operatic singer, was a guiding influence in the old car hobby in the late 1940s and helped to stir enthusiasm among collectors for the 50th anniversary.

Milwaukee in 1909 but, like Studebaker, traced its history farther back to carriage days. In 1919 Nash bought an interest in the company, the same year GM cemented its association with Fisher Body Company. Regarding Nash's 20-acre body plant in Milwaukee, company officials said, "It's ours, all ours, and we at Nash are proud of it." The company felt it was poised for postwar successes. Other independent auto makers held similar high hopes for the future.

The push to sell new cars in 1946 did not blind jubilee organizers to the involvement of old car hobbyists. On April 22, *Automotive News* reported that "an opportunity to highlight an international feature to the Automotive Golden Jubilee will be given in the addition of an extra day, May 29." This allowed for a large parade with numerous antique cars, many from 1915 and earlier. Some would be placed honorably on large floats fielded by various companies. The vehicles were then displayed at Convention Hall in Detroit. Radio was used to cover the jubilee events and the press was out in force: there were 50 photographers from publications and four cameramen from the newsreel

YOU'LL GO
HIGH, WIDE AND
HANDSOME—

There's a Ford in your future!

It will happen in the peacetime to come—when the tasks that now face America have been accomplished. Then a smart, new Ford will be waiting for you to drive it away.
. . . Trip after trip you'll cruise along in ease and style. It will be so smooth and gentle riding —always such a joy to handle.
. . . Here will be a car that's big and sturdy—plenty of room in front and back. It will be smartly styled. And for all its fleet and eager power, you will find this new car thrifty in the time-honored Ford tradition.
. . . That's how it will be. And when the "go ahead" is flashed, we'll be ready to start production plans. Meanwhile, the full Ford resources are helping to speed final Victory.

FORD MOTOR COMPANY

Ford

"THE FORD SHOW". Brilliant singing stars, orchestra and chorus. Every Sunday, NBC network. 2:00 P.M., E.W.T., 1:00 P.M., C.W.T., 12:00 M., M.W.T., 11:00 A.M., P.W.T.

When the anniversary came, Ford had already intrigued the public with its ad campaign on the crystal ball theme, "There's a Ford in Your Future."

producers. A newsreel preview of the parade was enacted in Franklin Village near Detroit with the first 1899 Packard on loan from Lehigh University leading the entourage. Even an 1896 Duryea was at the jubilee. Publicity photos were taken with current leaders of the industry in a 1902 Rambler, 1903 Cadillac, 1903 curved dash Oldsmobile, and the Packard.[8] John Conde recalled that the jubilee brought out the greatest grouping of early cars he would ever see!

Other sources acknowledged that 1946 was the golden anniversary year, too. The Golden Jubilee Year was marked by the reenactment of the Glidden Tour sponsored by the Veteran Motor Car Club of America. James Melton, popular operatic singer and antique car hobbyist, chaired the event committee and had the distinction of being at the wheel of a 1907 International Harvester Auto Wagon, which was the first antique car to be flown by modern aerial transportation from

1946 FORD
with many advancements
now in production!
There's a Ford in your future!
Here is the most beautiful Ford car ever built—with more improvements than many pre-war yearly models. . . . Under the broad hood there's new and greater power. Plus improved economy in oil and gasoline. . . . Colorful interiors invite you to relax in luxury. Plenty of elbow-room, knee-room, head-room. New-type springs assure a full-cushioned level ride. Brakes are new hydraulics—extra-large and self-centering—to make stops quick, smooth and quiet. . . . Ask your Ford Dealer about the smartest Ford cars ever built. FORD MOTOR COMPANY

When the new 1946 Fords rolled off the production line the image in the crystal ball revealed the beauty of the new car.

Small and large vintage vehicles chugged along the parade route, while more recent rare cars—such as the prewar Chrysler Imperial phaeton in foreground—contrasted the advancements of the auto industry.

Chicago to Newark, N.J., where the tour began. Even in Great Britain there was a celebration, July 18 through November 20, at which there were scale models, films, and historical displays about the 50th anniversary. It commemorated the opening of Britain's Motor Industry headquarters. From London the display made a swing through four British cities. A massive London Cavalcade, a parade of about 450 cars dating from 1896 to 1946, also was held.[9]

What lay ahead for the American auto industry in 1946 was great promise. It stood atop the world. As yet, there was no Germany or Japan with the ability to mass produce and market their cars worldwide. All signs pointed to the American automotive industry standing on the brink of major production and sales successes around the globe as never before.

At the time of the Golden Jubilee, Charles W. Nash said, "The pioneers who created the industry are glad to see that the men who have taken their places are carrying on in the same spirit. And that spirit says that pioneering is not something that was done only yesterday, but something that will remain as long as there is a need for a better way of doing things. With this spirit, America can count on the automobile industry to continue to help it move forward."

Notes

1. *THINK* Magazine, National Automotive Golden Jubilee Edition, International Business Machines Corp., New York, N.Y., 1946; pages 3 and 63. Various facts and figures from the magazine are used in this chapter.

2. *Carriages Without Horses, J. Frank Duryea and the Birth of the American Automobile Industry,* Richard P. Scharchburg, Society of Automotive Engineers, Warrendale, Pa., 1993; Chapter 1. In the May 16, 1931, edition of *The Saturday Evening Post,* Charles E. Duryea claimed he operated a gasoline vehicle as early as April 19, 1892, and had his first sales in the summer of 1896. He and his brother hotly disputed which one was really responsible for their first car. Charles' son, M. J. "Jerry" Duryea, would continue defending his father's rights against Frank's claims even in the late 1940s.

3. *Automobiles of America,* Automobile Manufacturers Association (AMA), Wayne State University Press, Detroit, 1970; page 199.

4. *Highlights of History, 25 Years with* MoToR, *1904-1929*; this hardbound, oversize book examined the industry in its first quarter century as revealed in the pages of the popular magazine. The numbering system is haphazard due to the reprint nature of the book; this quote comes from an installment running in the March 1909 issue of *MoToR.*

5. *THINK,* pages 4 and 5. Limits had to be put on the celebration. Who would be honored? Should homage be paid to all pioneers, including those no longer living, and would the organizers then run the risk of missing some? Based on these concerns, the 14 living pioneers became the focal point for the jubilee.

6. Two sources are used for this information: *Automotive News,* George M. Slocum, publisher, Detroit, April 22, 1946, page 2. Two photos appear with a short article about the jubilee. One photo is of the parade newsreel promotion and shows a line of about 20 vintage vehicles headed by the 1899 Packard. The short news story is by George B. Deery, staff writer. Also, some details and the quote come from John A. Conde in recollections recorded for Perschbacher, September 11, 1995.

7. Two sources are used for this information: "Automotive and Aviation Industries," News of the Industry, Automotive Division, Chilton Company, Philadelphia, July 1, 1946; page 50. And an original Kaiser-Frazer news release dated June 22, 1947.

8. *Automotive News,* April 22, 1946, page 2; One photo shows eight company heads seated in the four early automobiles, referenced in the main text. The officials are: George Mason (Nash), B. E. Hutchinson (Chrysler), C. E. Wilson (GM,) K. T. Keller (Chrysler), William S. Knudsen (jubilee committee and formerly of GM), Albert Bradley (GM), Alvan Macauley (Packard), and Robert Black (White).

9. *N.A.D.A. Magazine,* National Automobile Dealers Association, St. Louis and Washington, D.C., September 1946; page 18; and *Automotive and Aviation Industries,* Chilton Company, Philadelphia, Aug. 1, 1946; page 51.

Among early pioneer cars was the Winton. Alexander Winton built his experimental car in 1896 and in 1908 made his first six-cylinder car.

Little is known of certain car makers. While the Simplex Automobile Company made the popular Simplex in New York City and New Brunswick, N.J., and while there were two other companies under similar names that made a Simplex Steamer in Maine and the Derain in Ohio, not much is known of the Simplex Motor Car Company of Mishawaka, Ind. Some car makers cashed in on national publicity by taking on popular names for their company or car.

White made initial success with steam-powered cars beginning in 1900. The automotive effort was based on the financial strength of the White Sewing Machine and shows how companies diversified to meet the growing demand for cars.

The 1916 Apperson carried a V-8 engine and cost $1,850. The company's pioneers—Elmer and Edgar Apperson—had originally worked with Elwood Haynes but struck out on their own with the 1902 Apperson.

Elwood Haynes claimed to have built the first successful gasoline car in America in 1893. Many historians eventually settled on the Duryeas as holders of the claim.

The first 1901 Stevens-Duryea was built from a prototype by J. Frank Duryea, one of the industry's pioneers. The make ended production with the 1927 model.

One of the most popular early cars was the Overland, first made in Terra Haute, Ind., in 1903. The company moved to Indianapolis by 1905 and to Toledo, Ohio, for 1909.

"All Roads are Level to a Moyer" was the company slogan. The make was made from 1911 to 1915. Prices ranged near $3,000.

James Ward Packard, with the business acumen of his brother, William Doud Packard, took interest in a Winton and in 1899 made their first Packard car. They and subsequent company leaders—such as Henry B. Joy and Alvan Macauley—followed the formula for success.

Chapter 2

Formula for Success

"I think that within six to eight years 80 percent of vehicle traction in towns and cities in this country will be done by electricity," said Thomas Edison in June 1902.[1] But the first century of the automobile industry in America would prove the Wizard of Menlo Park to be wrong. The internal combustion engine became the mainstay.

There were challenges that faced the fledgling automobile industry at its inception in 1896. The formula for success carried five elements. The best combination of elements would determine longevity for car makes. It also would determine the very

Thomas A. Edison, right, served as an inspiration for Henry Ford, left, one of his employees prior to Ford's entry into auto production. In his later years, Edison found Ford to be a financial inspiration. The auto magnate loaned vast sums toward Edison's sometimes wild experiments, and very little was paid back. Even so, Ford appreciated the honor.

success of the industry, which was facing an uphill battle against mainline modes of transportation: the horse and wagon, the locomotive and trolley, and boats on major waterways.

The elements for success were simple: 1) Source of power; 2) Mass production; 3) Precision manufacturing; 4) Good distribution system; and 5) Meeting the needs of the public. The successful masterminds who blended the elements became the big wheels of industry who kept their business in motion. They were the X-factor of management.

Edison believed in the power of electricity as the future hope for civilization. By the late 1880s the phonograph, his favorite invention, was powered by electricity. He also made the electric light bulb commercially successful. Soon electric companies were springing up in a mad rush for business in major cities. Edison was among the early hopefuls, since he seldom invented anything that he could not make commercially profitable. He watched the automobile industry begin in America and discovered that the internal combustion engine was noisy, messy, and cantankerous. He also determined that the automobile business was worthy of pursuit. In the fall of 1903 he issued some startling news.

"AUTOS FOR THE POOR—Kind Mr. Edison is about to solve the transportation problem for the world," stated the *St. Louis Post-Dispatch* for October 6, 1903. "He pronounces that he has perfected a form of electrical energy which will supply automobiles with motive power and illuminate the house at the same time. His object, he declares, is to so cheapen the automobile as to place it in the hands of the masses. The machine which he has invented for supplying this energy or fuel for automobiles can be sold, he says, for $450. The long-suffering poor will rise up and call Mr. Edison blessed!"[2] Henry Ford, who had been an employee at the Edison Illuminating Company for several years, had to have taken notice of Edison's news. The idea of producing a car for the masses would stick with Ford and in 1908, with the introduction of the relatively cheap Model T Ford, would revolutionize the industry. However, he chose the internal combustion gasoline engine for success.

Some makers would investigate various sources of motive power. At Studebaker, the choice for electric power was not made quickly. In August of 1895, John M. Studebaker wrote: "We had already considered the possibility of adapting [the gasoline engine being made by Worth Manufacturing Company, Benton Harbor, Mich.] to a vehicle and we are giving the subject of horseless carriages very careful attention." Experimentation was conducted on a car by 1897 but the com-

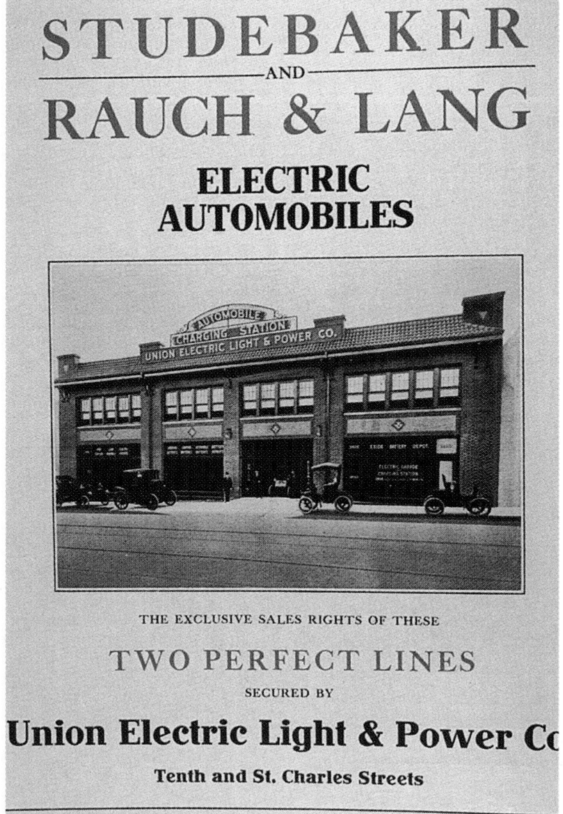

Studebaker and Rauch & Lang were makers of widely known electric cars and by 1907 were still clinging to this form of power. Studebaker would forsake electricity for gasoline engines after 1912. Rauch & Lang stuck with it until the company faltered in 1928.

The humorous side of the automobile was captured in period postcards. This early one is unusual since it promotes motoring by women.

pany concentrated instead on the supplying of bodies to electric car makers, thus remaining true to its wagon-building heritage. From 1902 to 1912 the Studebaker electric, based on a design by Edison, would be produced before the company shifted into production of internal combustion powered vehicles. Other makes of electric power seemed to abound early in the American automobile industry. Included were the Columbia (1897-1913), Riker (1897-1902), Baker (1899-1916), Buffalo (1901-1906 and 1912-1915), Rauch & Lang (1905-1928), and Detroit (1907 to circa 1939).[3]

What electricity offered was comparatively clean operation (although some owners quibbled about noxious fumes from the batteries), silent operation (horses and people weren't spooked, an especially safe and delightful option in big cities), and ease of driving (high speeds were basically beyond the capability of the electric car's gearing and batteries; it wasn't unusual for an electric car to go only about 20 or 25 mph at top speed). The cars had an unlimited source of fuel although long distance trips were unrealistic. Many electric cars could cover perhaps 40 or 50 miles at best before being recharged overnight. This was not a major hindrance for electric cars early in the 20th century, since very few roads connected cities, and fewer yet had surfacing. Most roads were wagon trails, often rutted, muddy when wet, and not at all pleasant for a Sunday drive.

As time went on, electric cars were made luxurious. By 1915

"Thoroughbred!" was the sales theme for this ad for the Ohio Electric. Ladies with large hats and stately apparel found the luxurious interiors of electric cars inviting.

Steam power had its adherents, a logical choice since steam locomotives had made history in opening the West in the late 1800s. This crude steam vehicle was said to have been made in 1890 and was typical of the efforts of numerous hopefuls who made their vehicles by hand at small shops in many larger American cities.

numerous luxury versions were built for a wealthy clientele and were fashioned after sitting rooms with fancy appointments. Electric cars were easy to start and were reliable in winter, although cold weather tended to sap power from the batteries. Some of the nation's earliest trucks were electric powered. They proved to be workhorses, although their speed seldom could run past 5 or 10 mph and they usually restricted their trade to a single city and its surrounding environs!

The pioneers didn't know it at first, but because the cars did not offer high speed or long distance performance their days were numbered. Industrialization had brought new wealth and ambition to America. With these came the demand for faster transport of goods to areas once restricted to horse and wagon due to rough terrain. The end of electric cars was hastened by the improvement of roads. As communities were linked by surfaced roadways, faster and longer trips became realistic.[4] Steam power

Facts about Early Cars

• Flywheels compensated for engine vibration. In 1907 designers determined these flywheel weights were needed for the elimination of vibration in various engines: six cylinder car, 20 lbs.; four, 90 lbs.; three, 200 lbs.; two, 400 lbs., and a one-cylinder engine needed a 1,000 lb. flywheel. "Vibration from even the 'one-lunger' can be practically eliminated but at an awful cost. . . by adding surplus weight." Hence, the days of multi-cylinder cars had arrived.[9]

• "Casualties in the battle between the two million people of Chicago and the 32,000 street cars, trains, teams [of horses], automobiles and other vehicles which pass through the streets amounted in first seven months of [1906] to: Killed, 259; injured, 2,671." Here was the breakdown: street cars killed 75 and injured 1,524; railroads killed 138, injured 420; teams of horses killed 39, injured 642; and autos killed seven, injured 85. Four of those car deaths were indirectly related. The automobile was being promoted as a safe means of transport.[10]

• The French word "chauffeur" originally meant a warming pan or foot warmer. "Robbers [in France] adopted the method of torturing the [occupants] of any house they entered by holding their feet in the fire until the hiding place of the family treasure was divulged. Hence, the name foot warmers was applied to them. From that it grew to mean a man who shovelled coal into a furnace and looked after the steam engine." In the early years of the American automobile industry when steam powered vehicles had to have their fires fed and engines adjusted, the term chauffeur took on renewed meaning. The term eventually was applied to the paid driver of a gasoline motor car since he not only took passengers to their destinations but also cared for the vehicle.[11]

• In 1895 the U.S. Patent Office granted George Selden, a patent attorney with a mechanical interest, a patent for his 1879 version of a motor car with a gasoline-fueled internal combustion engine. The Association of Licensed Automobile Manufacturers issued permission for use based on the patent if a firm could show it was in a position to invest $200,000 in the production of motor cars. The patent resulted in litigation against any car maker that used this motive form without paying royalties. Henry Ford's company was the most at risk due to the mass production of the Model T Ford and became the focus of the patent fight. In 1909 the patent was sustained against Ford. He fought while other car makers paid fees under the patent. Ford continued his court battle and won his appeal in 1911. With this victory, the patent monopoly came to a close and an unrestricted future favored the industry.[12]

• Most of the early automotive big wheels had emerged from the bicycle industry, "a $60 million industry with 250 manufacturing establishments in 1896 when there were more than four million riders of two-wheelers."[13]

was a logical choice for the fledgling auto makers. Locomotives had chugged their way through much of the 19th century under steam and had opened the Wild West. Because of locomotives the industrial products of the East Coast wended southward and westward to expanded markets. So why shouldn't steam be applied to the motor car?

Among early entries in the category were Francis E. and Freeland O. Stanley, identical twin brothers who took a liking to steam. Their first experience was successfully launched in 1897, but they sold their business interests for $250,000. A squabble between John Brisben Walker, publisher of *Cosmopolitan* magazine, and Amzi Lorenzo Barber, his financier in the Stanley buy-out, resulted in the production of the Mobile steam car from 1900 to 1903 and the Locomobile, which began in 1899 as a steam-powered vehicle. Meanwhile, the Stanleys formed another company to make a car by their name from 1901-1927 in Newton, Mass.

"An ordinary Mobile, just out of the factory stockroom, was driven by Mr. Frank Lambkin of Norwalk, Ohio, from Kingland Point (Tarrytown-on-the-Hudson in New York, where Mobiles were made) to Chicago without breakage, interruption, or perceptible wear and tear of any kind. This same Mobile after being driven over 4,000 miles was sold by Mr. Lambkin for the full price of a new Mobile," said the company in 1901. Another Mobile had steamed its way from Colorado Springs, Colo., to the timberline of Pike's Peak, an upward drive of 25 miles and 10,000 feet above sea level, over a practically abandoned wagon trail. A Mobile took the Vanderbilt Cup in racing in September 1900, said the auto maker. Owners noted that 60 miles travel in one day was not uncommon, and that the machine "can be operated successfully by any person, man or woman, who will familiarize themselves with it."[5] An electric car could never hope to match such rugged performance. The drawback to steam was the consideration of safety (many people feared the boiler would blow up) and long warm-up time preliminary to operation (some early steamers took 20 minutes or more to fire up before driving).

Although his methods of industrialization and mass production in the late 1800s were patterned by others, Edison wasn't the only role model who gave the automobile industry inspiration. There was one man in Michigan who had come to the forefront. And he pursued the gasoline internal combustion engine as the power plant of choice.

Ransom E. Olds had envisioned the success of private motorized transportation. P. F. Olds & Son was among the largest makers of gasoline engines in central Michigan, and interests turned

The 1904 auto show in New York brought together a variety of vehicles of different makes. By 1930 many of those manufacturers had become history.

toward making their own cars. In 1897 the Olds Motor Vehicle Company in Lansing, Mich., was formed. Ransom Olds had been tinkering with motorized contraptions for about a decade and now was ready to reap results. From 1899 to 1900 he made only about 11 different cars and there was some work done with electrics. Then a fire devastated the plant on March 9, 1901. Only one gasoline runabout was saved, a curved dash model. It became the torchbearer and early milestone for gasoline cars in America, since it served as a pattern for the first mass-produced car in the country. In 1901 production of the one model reached 425; for 1902, 2,500; 1903, 4,000; and 1904, 5,508. At $650 the little gasoline motorcar was far out-distancing the production of its more costly competition.[6]

In 1900 gasoline generally was considered too volatile to store and was discarded as an unfit byproduct from the refinement of crude oil for home and business use. But for the automobile it was the right octane fuel source, easily stored in a tank. As the gasoline car increased in production, so did the demand for its fuel. The oil companies had found a new source of revenue.

A few companies offered all three types of motive transportation. Colonel Albert Pope, who had served on the staff of

Dealerships sought prime locations, mainly in the downtown districts of large cities or along heavily traveled streets and roads that led downtown. Here is a 1907 view of the Reyburn Motor Company, St. Louis, Mo.

Interior view of the Reyburn dealership, which handled Stearns and Royal gasoline cars and the Babcock Electric. Due to brick and wood construction in early buildings, fire was a common danger to dealerships and brought ruin to many.

General Ulysses S. Grant, had converted his bicycle business into car production. He was among the earliest big wheels in the industry. The Duryea brothers even considered going into business with him. Pope felt the horse's days were numbered. By 1899 his plants in Hartford, Conn., were out-producing all other American makers combined. His efforts produced more than half of all new cars in the United States in 1899. Of 1,661 steam cars made that year, he produced 1,191. Among the 1,575 electric cars, Pope accounted for 734. Of gasoline vehicles, Pope claimed 171 out of 936. Most other companies making steam, gas, or electric cars usually produced from 25 to less than 200 vehicles. Pope was making more cars than all of them combined. However, a severe recession struck in 1908, and with the sinking of his bicycle business Pope's empire would collapse into receivership. At the 1900 automobile show at Madison Square Garden in New York, "eight companies exhibited electric vehicles; five companies exhibited gasoline automobiles; and two companies exhibited steam automobiles." Some of the bigger auto makers did not show their cars, believing "that other methods of advertising and acquainting the public with their automobiles were more satisfactory." The fact that the same site had become a popular place for a spring electric show possibly attracted the electric car makers.[7] Gasoline cars were the real success story. At the Fifth National Automobile Show at Madison Square Garden in 1905, there would be 177 gasoline cars on display, compared to 31 electrics and only four steamers.[8]

When it came to the American automobile and its industrial leadership, wheels were in motion as never before!

Notes

1. *St. Louis Post-Dispatch*, June 8, 1902.

2. Ibid., Oct. 6, 1903; Edison's new storage battery was to power his electric cars, but he did not become an auto maker. He told reporters that he intended to "put the horse out of business." He claimed his battery would take a car 100 miles before recharging. Also, for the impact Edison had on Henry Ford and industrial production techniques, see *Edison, A Biography*, Matthew Josephson, McGraw-Hill Book Company, Inc., New York, 1959.

3. *Standard Catalog of American Cars, 1805-1942*, Beverly Rae Kimes and Henry Austin Clark, Jr., Krause Publications, Iola, Wis., 1985; see entries as noted. Also, *Who? What? When? Where? Automotive Chronological Calendar*, Bob Francis, 1108 West Jackson, Tupelo, Miss. 38801; 1994. The Studebaker quote and certain miscellaneous facts elsewhere in the text occasionally use this as a source.

4. *Driving Passion*, a four-hour video production by Turner Home Entertainment, Atlanta, Ga., 1995. This serious and entertaining production includes numerous comments from primary sources and automotive historians.

5. *The Automobile*, E. L. Powers Co., New York, N.Y.; quotes are taken from a four-page advertising supplement on Mobile in the November 1900 edition.

6. *Standard Catalog of American Cars, 1805-1942*, see Oldsmobile entry.

7. *The Automobile*, February 1900, page 22.

8. Statistics derived from *Birth of a Giant. . .* , Crabb, pp. 35-37, and *Automobiles of America*, AMA, page 36.

9. *The Auto Review*, Automobile Club of St. Louis, St. Louis, Mo., January 1907, page 26.

10. Ibid., page 27.

11. Ibid., May 1907, page 75.

12. *Automobiles of America*, Automobile Manufacturers Association, Wayne State University Press, Detroit, Mich., 1970; pp. 13, 47, 52, and 215; also, *Birth of a Giant, The Men and Incidents that Gave America the Motorcar*, Richard Crabb, Chilton Book Company, Philadelphia, Pa., 1969; pp. 121 & 122.

13. Comment by Walter Bermingham, historian of the 1939 Chicago Automobile Show, *Automobile Book of the Year, 1939, An Age of Wheelprints*, Chicago Automobile Trade Association.

The Evolution of Frontal Styling

The curved dash Oldsmobile of 1901-1904 took the appearance of a glorified horseless carriage with its dash board, which originally protected carriage riders against offensive mud and stones hurled from the road by horse hooves.

The Model A Ford of 1903 put the radiator out front and stylized the dash area.

Around 1910 the traditional radiator had developed as a major emphasis to the frontal styling of cars, as typified by this Maxwell. The forward engine compartment necessitated a hood.

By the late 1920s, even air-cooled Franklins had taken on "radiator styling" in hopes to gain buyers who liked a conventional appearance.

In 1932, Packard took styling a step farther with a rakish taper and slant to its Light Eight.

Duesenberg styling for 1932 had made the long pointed hood a fashion expression with a massive chromed radiator-grille assembly.

By 1937 the grille assembly became a key part of a car's appearance, as seen on this Cadillac. By freeing the radiator from the grille, designers became creative in lowering the silhouette and establishing new styling motifs, which equated to better sales.

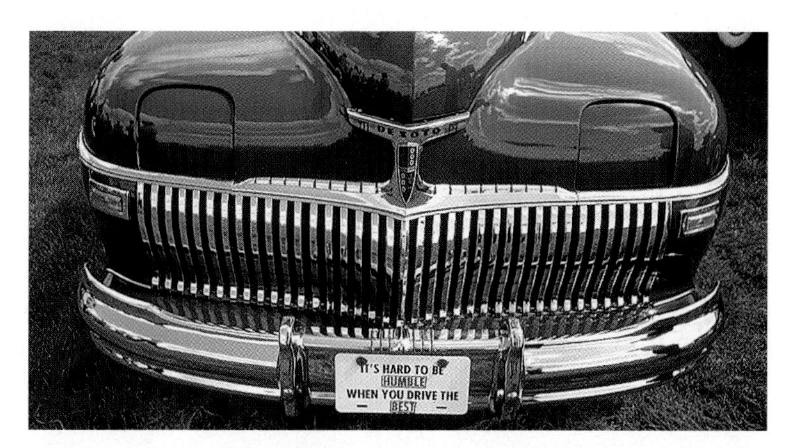

By 1942, hideaway headlights had been sported by Cord (1936-1937) and DeSoto, pictured here. Grilles took on massive proportions.

For 1950 the grille had been changed into THE styling statement for the public's first view of a car. This 1950 Buick offered a unique blend of grille and bumper guard assembly.

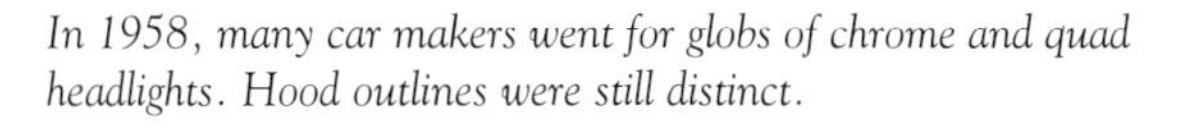

In 1958, many car makers went for globs of chrome and quad headlights. Hood outlines were still distinct.

As the 1960s were ready to dawn, the fronts of cars took on jet-like resemblance.

Around 1910 city streets hardly welcomed motorized transportation. Some cities maintained speed limits of 10 or 15 mph. Large, slow moving cars contended with horse-drawn wagons along crowded byways.

Chapter 3

Fascination with Motion

"It was about the end of the 19th century that Big Business decided to take hold of the horseless carriage. . . license plates and operator's licenses began to appear. The motor-propelled vehicle ceased to be a novelty. The glory of the early pioneering faded." Such was the assessment of Hiram Percy Maxim in 1937. The inventor of the Maxim silencer for guns also had been an automotive pioneer in Hartford, Conn., and had worked with gasoline and electric cars. For him, the 1900s marked an end to the freedom of wheels that had been set in motion. Now big wheels in business had captured the industry.[1]

Among the industry leaders was Ransom E. Olds. With the outpouring of his new curved dash Oldsmobiles from 1901-1904 Ransom E. Olds offered mass production to the formula for success. Although the moveable assembly line concept would be added to the industrial equation in great measure by Henry Ford, it was Olds who became the first big wheel in the movement of the American automobile industry. Since Olds based his production in Lansing, Mich., he proved something else: Detroit wasn't automatically the capital of American automobile production.[2]

By 1902 there were more than 200 firms which could be considered active in automobile production. Of those, only five had annual production exceeding 100: the Olds Motor Works based in Lansing; the Winton Motor Company in Cleveland, Ohio; the Thomas B. Jeffery Company, Kenosha, Wis., which made the Rambler; the Pope Manufacturing Company, Hartford, Conn., making the Columbia; Apperson Brothers Machine Shop, Kokomo, Ind., makers of the Haynes-Apperson. Many companies had a difficult time securing financing since most major

Opposite, bottom: The Fisher Body Plant in Flint, Mich., was typical of the large facilities that GM and other mass producers of cars had to operate in order to maintain volume production.

Hard-to-reach places became touring destinations for cars. With the desire to travel, more roads were being oiled to keep down dust and water erosion and surfaced to offer better rides and faster speeds.

In 1896 Duryea led production with 13 cars. It wasn't until 1898 that 100 cars were made by one manufacturer—Stanley. Winton came in second with 22 units. In 1899 an estimated 500 Columbia cars were made, 400 Locomobiles, and 100 Wintons. Columbia held the lead with about 1,500 cars for 1900, with Locomobile staying in second with about 750. In 1901 Locomobile held the lead with around 1,500 cars, Oldsmobile held second with 425, and White was third with 193. In 1902, the Locomobile steamer marked the final success story for that type of power plant with 2,750 cars sold. Oldsmobile took second place, White was a distant third with 385. Oldsmobile would hold the lead in production until it was unseated by Ford in 1906.[8]

Sporting an all-steel body was unusual in 1917, but cars by Dodge Brothers promoted this practical method of construction. Dodges also predicted the prevailing use of the 12-volt electrical system, which the make already carried in 1914. In 1915 Dodge ran third in production behind Ford and Willys-Overland and in 1920 was second to Ford.

banks in the East or Midwest hesitated to provide credit unless companies had other resources—such as Studebaker with its established wagon trade.

As World War I raged in Europe, there were makers in many states. More than a few states had notable concentrations of auto makers. New York claimed Franklin, Pierce-Arrow, Palmer-Singer, and Simplex; other eastern states such as Pennsylvania and Massachusetts also had active auto makers. Ohio had Packard (until it moved to Detroit in 1903), Peerless, Stearns, Stoddard-Dayton, and International (a popular highwheeler model that looked more like a horseless wagon than an automobile). Indiana was home to Auburn, Marmon, McFarlan, Overland, National, Stutz, Haynes, Apperson, Studebaker, Waverley Electric, and others. Until 1905, Indianapolis alone had more auto makers than Detroit. Wisconsin claimed Mitchell, Maibohm, Rambler, and later Jeffery and Nash. In the early 1900s some makes branched out and called several states home. Maxwell was made in New York, Indiana, Rhode Island, and finally Michigan. Some makers were found west of Kansas

The improved reliability of motor vehicles resulted in their increased use for emergencies.

City, Mo., but the concentration was heaviest in the Midwest and the East. By 1909, Flint, Mich., on the strength of Buick production, would be considered the fastest growing industrial city in the country.[3]

St. Louis was a central location for car manufacturing. Research has uncovered about 100 marques made there. Among the most influential industry personalities was George P. Dorris, who engineered the St. Louis from 1899-1905 and the Dorris from 1906-26. He had built his first two-cylinder car in 1895 in Nashville, Tenn., and in 1898, with John L. French, set up the St. Louis business that was reported in 1907 to be "the fourth manufacturer in the field, first to adopt the sliding gear transmission." Dorris was responsible for other mechanical improvements that resulted in the motor, clutch, and transmission being built as a single unit. Additional innovations by Dorris became industry standards and were much admired by other automotive pioneers. A. L. Dyke, also in St. Louis, set up the first mail order parts business in 1899 and went on to make his own car. He also was credited with inventing the first American made carburetor

Scientific American reported on January 30, 1904: "Our leading manufacturers have moved up to the front rank, and are turning out machines that compare in design, workmanship, and beauty with the very best of foreign make. . . . But now that the period of experiment is over, and the growing confidence of the public in the automobile is resulting in a remarkable growth of the industry, we are witnessing a rush of inexperienced and often completely unqualified people into the trade. . . with the result that a lot of crude machines, which are made up largely of poor imitations of standard makes, are being offered to the public, long before they have had that exhaustive trial which alone can establish them as fit for the severe demands of everyday service on the road. Of course, these mushroom firms will, in most cases, meet with the inevitable fate of such; but not until many an inexperienced purchaser has paid dearly. . . ."[9]

William C. (Billy) Durant (left), made Buick No. 1, and then founded General Motors. David Dunbar Buick, (right), founder of Buick.

of float-feed design which became widely used in the industry. H. F. Borbein made running gears, axles, steering mechanisms, pressed steel or angle iron frames, and bodies for various makes.

A motorcade of 59 cars drove from New York to St. Louis for the 1904 World's Fair to participate in "Automobile Day." The succeeding year the Glidden Tour was held as a direct result.

Like other major cities, many of the local makes had short duration but a few registered good sales, were active nationally in advertising, and gained memorable reputations. The successful Moon and Gardner would be made in St. Louis. The fact that St. Louis had become a transportation gateway between east and west, north and south, made it a natural as a production site and also as an oil refinement location and distribution point. In 1949 the oil industry saluted St. Louis as the home of the first gasoline station built in 1905 solely for the purpose of servicing automobiles. Such automotive activity attracted the attention of officials with Ford and Chevrolet, and plants were established in St. Louis before World War I. For a major portion of the American auto industry's first century, Missouri—and specifically St. Louis—figured as second only to Michigan and Detroit as car

Coupe's (pronounced koo-pays') had been popular with professionals, such as doctors. With the use of the electric self-starter in the teens, women also took to the body style.

Towns with large main streets offered parking havens for cars in the center of the thoroughfare. The touring car was the body style most preferred.

production centers. More than anything, Detroit was brought forward as the center of motorcar production due mainly to a large labor pool, access to raw materials via the Great Lakes, and the rise of the mass produced Model T Ford, plus contributions by Cadillac, Lincoln, Hudson, Dodge, Packard, Maxwell, and Chalmers, among others.[4]

William C. Durant set a trend for the future with his foresight in forming a conglomerate. In January of 1908 he and Benjamin Briscoe met with Ford and Olds to explore combining Buick, Ford, Maxwell-Briscoe, and Reo. Each of these companies had an annual production of about 8,000 vehicles and stood far atop the heap of auto makers. The new company would have dominated the industry. But Ford and Olds wanted to sell their businesses outright for cash rather than be involved in a new corporation and the issuing of stock. Later that year, undaunted, Durant formed General Motors by starting with Buick, then adding a multitude of marques in a patchwork-quilt pattern of growth: Cadillac, Oldsmobile, Oakland, Carter, Elmore, Ewing, Welch, Little, and others. Some of the acquisitions proved financially bothersome and contributed to Durant's departure in 1910.

A middle-aged Henry Ford smiles beside his best-known invention, the Model T. It was this low-priced, no-frill, simple car that allowed many Americans to own their own wheels. In the early years of the 1900s, Ford's system of distribution and service was among the strongest in the industry and positioned the company for success.

Mass production, which was favored by the Oldsmobile early in the century, was taken forward in a giant step by the Model T Ford. Car makers were keenly examining ways in which higher volume could be attained without increasing expenses.

The Model T Ford made its mark on rural America as a helper in farm work.

But he would be back.

The Ford Motor Company began with respectable production levels. Key to the company's future was high production at low cost and what Ford officials called "flow production whereby the flow of components is regulated through every manufac-

The automobile had become Americanized in 1906. Prior to that year, exports had not been reliably recorded, which indicates that they very likely were insignificant figures. Cars imported to the United States totaled 26 for 1901; 265 for 1902; 267 for 1903; 605 for 1904; and 1,054 for 1905. In 1906, there were 1,106 cars imported and 1,850 exported. By 1912 imports had dwindled to 868 against a mammoth 23,720 for export![10]

Even good roads that meandered through mountains challenged the pulling power and carburetion of cars before 1920.

turing process." In the 1903 calendar year, production reached 1,708. That figure was passed in 1906 with 8,729, which put the make in top place, unseating Oldsmobile. It would hold first place uncontested until Chevrolet edged ahead in 1931. Henry Ford had finally settled on a low-priced offering for success, and in 1907 production for the company reached 14,887. It dipped to 10,202 for 1908, but then the Model T Ford was introduced. The industry was to be changed forever. In the 1909 calendar year, production rose to 17,771, past the 32,000 mark for 1910, and almost 68,000 units for 1911. Then some astronomical increases took place: 170,211 for 1912; 202,667 for 1913; 308,162 for 1914; and the 500,000 mark was surpassed for 1915. In 1916, 734,811 Ford Model Ts were made. For 1922, the million-car level would be passed for a single year's production! Ford was far outselling the rest of the automobile industry in America.[5]

At the introduction of the Model T Ford in 1908, the auto industry had taken a divergent approach to pricing. New York City hosted two major auto shows that year, at Madison Square Garden and Grand Central Palace. The breakdown of models by price is interesting. Totals for the shows had 25 models on display selling for less than $1,000; 35 models from $1,000 to $1,999; 33 models from $2,000 to $2,999; 38 models from $3,000 to $3,999;

The January 1908 edition of *Motor Age* noted: "Whatever may have been the success of the foreign car in America it is apparent that its days as a material factor in competition here are numbered." It went on to say that "foreign cars will always be sold in America, but the number will grow so small that in a year or so the profits that may be derived from their sales will barely keep alive a couple of agencies." This observation was to hold true into the 1950s.

The Essex was introduced by Hudson for 1919 and would remain in production until 1932. In the car's early history, racing events proved its 55 hp performance. In a 1919 endurance run, an Essex was driven for 50 hours at an average speed just over 60 mph.

and 39 models at $4,000 and over. For both shows, the four cylinder car dominated with 109 models vs. 31 "sixes."[6] Even $1,000 was a substantial amount for 1908; a small house could be bought for that price! Mass production techniques and cost controls would cover another element for success: getting the price of new cars down to the level of affordability for more buyers, thus meeting a need of the broader public.

Mass production wasn't enough for success. What the Model T offered was good manufacturing, too. And when it came to that element of success, the entire industry took off its hat to Henry Leland.

Leland had made his fame in industry before he began production for Cadillac, a reformed company from an earlier Ford venture. At the machine shop of Leland, Faulconer (a wealthy lumberman), and Norton (a tool designer) in Detroit during the 1890s, precision standards were upheld in the manufacturing of parts. Olds had come to the firm for his transmissions and engines after initial efforts to make them himself. He had also been buying engines from John and Horace Dodge. The Leland parts worked quieter, meshed better, and had the edge in performance and workmanship. But as consultant for Cadillac, Leland

The Marmon Wasp took the top honor at the first Indianapolis 500 race held in 1911. The racing business was becoming a professional offshoot of the car industry.

found a free hand for his genius and hard work.

Introduced on October 17, 1902, Cadillac precision construction enthralled buyers. At the New York Automobile Show held soon after, orders for 2,286 Cadillacs were placed. Actual calendar year production for 1903 reached 1,698, which placed Cadillac in third place behind Oldsmobile and Ford, and just ahead of Pope Hartford and Rambler. Cadillac went to second place in production in 1904 and retained its place for 1905 with 4,059 units. Still, Leland's greatest achievement was yet to be proved.

In 1908, in Great Britain, the Dewar Trophy was awarded to Cadillac. It was the result of three identical models having been disassembled, their parts jumbled, and then reassembled under the scrutiny of impartial judges. Each car was able to run under its own power after the ordeal. Such precision workmanship of parts brought the industry to a crossroads of quality. And Leland led the way. Had the interchangeability of parts not taken place for the industry, not only would mass production have been hindered in its advance, but the reliability of the American automobile would have suffered considerably.

Standardization had to be taken one step further. Standards needed to be set between all makes. For example, by 1910 one

Notable firsts took place before 1920. A Winton was the first car to cross the country in 1903, taking 44 days. The first motor vehicle track races were held in September of 1896 at Narragansett Park, R.I. (most spectators were "bored," a reporter noted). The first insurance policy for the operation of a car was issued in February 1898 to Dr. Truman J. Martin of Buffalo, N. Y., by Traveler's Insurance Co., for a premium of $11.05. The first auto show was held in November of 1900 at Madison Square Garden, New York City. In 1908 a Thomas Flyer was the first American car to gain world recognition in performance and dependability by winning the New York to Paris automobile race—a 13,341 mile and 88 day contest (the car went an average of 151 miles per day). By 1908 Maxwells were being actively promoted by Cadwallader W. Kelsey, sales manager, who persuaded Alice H. Ramsey and three of her lady friends to take the first cross-country trip by women from New York to San Francisco in 1909. The first motor truck to cross the country was a 1912 Packard with a three-ton load. And the first cars were allowed to enter Yosemite National Park in August of 1913.

For 1913 the Buick Model 24 cost $950 in roadster form; 2,850 were made. The money winner in top sales for Buick that year was the Model 31 three-door touring car for five passengers. It sold for $1,285 and 10,000 were produced.

The American truck industry was related to the automobile industry. In 1900, for only $100, a man could buy a horse and wagon and be in the transport business. Railroads shipped most of the necessary commodities between cities. But with motorized transport, trucks gained in favor. They were first limited to urban use. As road conditions improved, the heavy haulers began to make cautious treks between cities. The trustworthiness of trucks in World War I hastened their use in America as the troops returned home with tales of the truck's performance.

Car makers also supplied trucks. In 1898 Winton was making a delivery wagon, actually a converted gasoline automobile with truck body. White was in the steam car and truck business in 1900 by also producing a delivery wagon. Henry Ford tried his hand at making his first van in 1900 and would follow in 1908 with a one-ton truck based on the Model T.

One and two-cylinder gas-powered deliveries were built by the St. Louis Motor Carriage Company in 1901. In 1902, Studebaker, the wagon-building company it was, logically entered the truck business. Reo began its truck making in 1904. The company that would become Autocar built its first truck in 1899. In 1902 Rapid built a cab-over-engine truck. Mack had its beginning in the bus business in 1902. Diamond T entered the business in 1905, Federal in 1910, International Harvester in 1907.[11]

parts maker was producing 800 different sizes of lock washers, 1,600 sizes of steel tubing, and 135 different types of steel alloy. The Mechanical Branch of the Association of Licensed Automobile Manufacturers and the Society of Automotive Engineers brought order from chaos. The 800 sizes of lock washers were standardized to 16. The 1,600 steel tube sizes were dropped to 210. And the types of steel alloy were reduced to less than 50. By standardizing such simple parts, not only did it help in repairs but it also brought the cost factor down for the car makers, which in turn was be passed to the buyer![7]

With the arrival of precision manufacturing, the industry had achieved the third element in the formula for success. Now automobile owners did not need to worry about having replacement parts machined special for their new cars. Trust in the automobile was gained. An entire sub-industry could flourish: the parts business. Local dealers could service cars with less cost and better certainty in results. Even factory-issued warranties became viable.

But was there a good distribution system for new cars and their repair? Were the needs of the public being met? Had the final elements in the formula for success been discovered?

Notes

1. *Horseless Carriage Days*, Hiram Percy Maxim, Harper & Brothers Publishing, New York, N.Y., and London, England, 1937; page 162.

2. Charles E. Duryea said, "The real epoch-making Olds effort was begun in 1899 when he saw the failure of the steamers before others did and produced this car to fill their market. . . . H.T. Thomas, Marr, Coffin, and many others since prominent in the industry gained their first experience on these cars. . . . Many believe that this car should have grown into the business since taken by Ford and that Olds' separation from the Oldsmobile Co. (in 1904) was due to a difference of opinion as to the future market." *Highlights of History, 25 Years with* MoToR, *1904-1929*, from article titled, "Should Auld Acquaintance be Forgot" by Duryea, appearing in the January 1918 edition of *MoToR*.

3. A breakdown on the early car makers is offered in chapter seven of *Birth of a Giant, The Men and Incidents that Gave America the Motorcar*, Richard Crabb, Chilton Book Company, Philadelphia, 1969. *Standard Catalog of American Cars, 1805-1942*, Kimes & Clark, shows the dates of manufacture and production locations of a multitude of makes. Numerous cars were made in Illinois. More than 280 were made in the Chicago area, including American Electric, Ames Steamer, Auto Wagon, Banker, Barton Steamer, Benson, Coey Flyer, C.F., the Chicago Electric, King, Pioneer, Sears, Star, Ward, Woods Electric, and Yellow.

4. The 270 page book *Four Wheels No Brakes* produced by the St. Louis Society-Automobile Pioneers, 1930, lists 29 makes of cars made in St. Louis. Original copies of the book are rare, so it was reprinted by Auto Review Publishing, P.O. Box 510, Florissant, Mo., 63032. About 100 makes were issued from this city. Historian John A. Conde adds that it was the mass production of the Model T Ford that really put Detroit into the forefront.

5. The quote about "flow production" is taken from *Scrapbook of Ford in England*, a promotional motion picture for Ford use in 1960; courtesy, Harold J. Doebel. Figures in this section taken from *The Production Figure Book for U.S. Cars*, Jerry Heasley, Motorbooks International, Osceola, Wis., 1977; page 33.

6. *Highlights of History, 25 Years with* MoToR, *1904-1929*; entry titled, "The Motor Car of 1909," January 1909 issue of *MoToR*.

7. Cadillac comments are based in part on *Cadillac, the Complete Seventy-Year History*, Maurice D. Hendry, Automobile Quarterly Publications, L. Scott Bailey, Publisher, Princeton Publishing Inc., Princeton, N.J., 1973; pp. 18-26. Comments about standardization of small parts and alloys comes from *The Automobile Industry, Its Economic & Commercial Development*, Ralph C. Epstein, A.W. Shaw Company, Chicago, 1928; page 41.

8. Figures condensed from *The American Car Since 1775*, by the editors of *Automobile Quarterly*, L. Scott Bailey, Publisher, New York, N.Y., 1971; pp. 138 & 139.

9. *Scientific American*, Munn & Co., New York, N.Y., Jan. 30, 1904; page 74, "Mushroom Automobile Firms" (courtesy of Ralph Atkinson).

10. *America Adopts the Automobile, 1895-1910*, James J. Flick, The MIT Press, Cambridge, Mass., 1970; page 60.

11. *Pictorial History of American Trucks*, Niels Jansen, Bay View Books, Bideford, Devon, England; 1994; pp. 9-13.

Long ago a collector of car badges pried this one from a car in a junkyard. The Maxim Motor Company of Middleboro, Mass., was headed by C. W. Maxim. It was reported in 1902 that Maxim was entering the car business, but few evidently were built.

The McFarlan, made from 1910 to 1928 in Connersville, Ind., was an outgrowth of the McFarlan Carriage Company as that business turned toward motorized transport. Initial price was $2,000 and this was raised to a whopping $6,000 by 1920. Its best year was 1922, with 235 cars sold!

The ReVere, named after the Revolutionary War hero, was made from 1918 to 1926. It was introduced at $3,850. Using the four-cylinder Duesenberg engine, the car was a hot and sporty performer.

Introduced on Washington's birthday in February of 1921 and lasting into 1924, the Washington automobile was made in Ohio. Called "The Ideal of a Nation," this assembled car was the result of businessmen from various sectors pooling their financial resources.

Like many car pioneers, Charles H. Metz was successful in the bicycle business, making as many as 15,000 in 1897. He became editor of Cycle and Automobile Trade Journal *in 1901, and from 1909 to 1921 made the Metz.*

From Cleveland came the Templar, made from 1917 to 1924. A well designed assembled car, its engine was noteworthy: an overhead valve four with valves housed in an aluminum case. It displaced 197 cubic inches and put out 43 hp. By the end of 1919 about 1,800 Templars had been built.

"Made in the West; Built for the World" was the slogan for the Patriot of Lincoln, Neb., which was offered in truck form from 1920 to 1926.

The Little was part of William C. Durant's second automotive empire in 1912 and 1913. It was named after William H. Little, Durant's former general manager at Buick. It was a simple, low-cost car selling at $690. Durant combined many features into Chevrolet and discontinued the Little name.

Carrying capacities of early cars was limited. Wicker baskets, placed at the rear or alongside the passenger compartment, allowed some degree of storage without impeding on passengers.

Metal boxes, especially for carrying tools and necessary items in the event of a breakdown, appeared at the rear by 1910. Early touring cars also allowed for cargo space under the rear seat cushion.

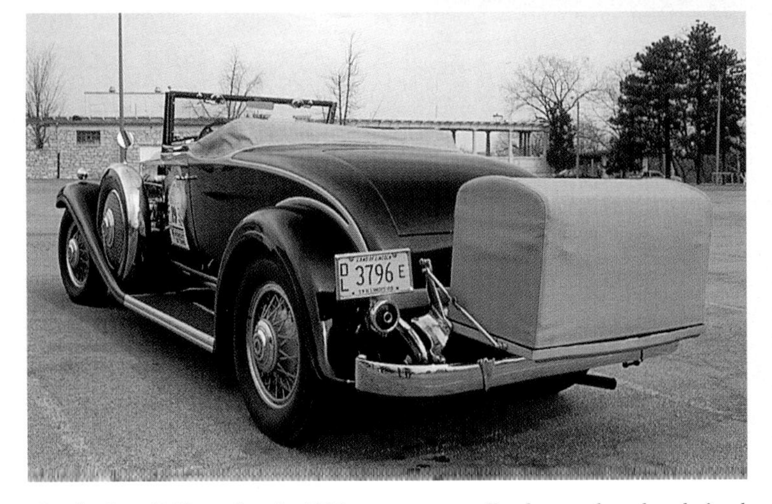

By the late 1920s and early 1930s, many cars offered a trunk and rack fitted specially to a make. Among the last car makers to carry such an option was Packard in the early 1940s.

Built-in trucks became popular on coupes in the late 1920s, but would not become a regular part of most four-door sedans until the mid-1930s.

Chapter 4

The Automobile and Its Dealers Take Modern Form

The basic form of the American automobile had taken shape by 1920. Fenders, wheels, steering principles, motor design, interior configuration, and other features had been established for the overall effective function of the passenger car. Even crude automatic transmissions had been designed.

The prevailing body style of 1919, which accounted for nearly 90 percent of all production, was the open car, in roadster, touring, or phaeton forms. By the end of the 1920s, the open car's production share would come to about 8 percent—a complete reversal in a decade.

Matters regarding the source of fuel, mass production, and interchangeability of precision parts generally had been decided by the late teens and early twenties. To complete the formula for success, the industry needed a good and active system of distribution and a way of meeting the needs of the public.

> Nashes to Nashes, Stutz to Stutz;
> If the Buicks don't get you
> The Chevrolets must.

So went a popular poem in 1925. It typified the ongoing advances of large auto makers that were marked in that decade. While Nash and Stutz had good sales organizations, those of Buick and Chevrolet seemed to be better.

"I don't suppose you know anything about (the crocodile and) his habits, and so I am going to tell you his chief failing," the Chevrolet Motor Company of Kansas City told its dealers as the 1920s approached. "He hasn't any energy at all. Lazy? Yes, but it seems that he deserves a stronger name than that. When the tide washes him ashore, do you think he tries to get back in the water? He does not. He waits until the water reaches him again. In this respect, the crocodile reminds us of some humans.

In 1923 "the oldest car in America in actual continuous service" was an 1899 Mobile steamer. The fact was authenticated by the National Automobile Chamber of Commerce. The two-cylinder car was of 4 hp and had 298 ½ tubes in the boiler. Steam pressure was 125-180 lbs. and its speed was 12 mph. "I am combining the fun of driving the old kettle with a profitable business of soliciting subscriptions for the *American Automobile Digest*,'" said John M. Barr of Dayton, Ohio, who owned the car. The Mobile had been driven almost 200,000 miles.[10]

They wait for something to happen. Instead of using energy, and forcing themselves into the thick of business, they wait and hope for business to come to them. And while they are pursuing this policy, the energetic, keen business man is getting the business." Although the views of the crocodile were simplistic, the point was serious: Chevrolet dealers were called to action![1]

What was surfacing across America was a system of dealers who not only offered sales outlets for the public but also service facilities. The auto makers that vigorously pursued this logic had the next element for the formula of success.

The Chevrolet "490" was introduced as a 1916 model and was William C. Durant's attempt to gain a stronghold in the low-price field. Durant, deposed as the power broker of General Motors, which he had founded in 1908, had begun Chevrolet in 1911 on the magic of the name and reputation of race car driver Louis Chevrolet. Cars that the company made prior to the 490 sold from $750 to $2,500 and were no threat to the Model T Ford, which had gained relatively astronomical sales achievements by 1916. Durant saw weaknesses in the Model T, in that the cars were crude in design and offered little more than basic transportation. With the 490 he hoped to offer more in styling, ease of operation, and modest luxury. He made his goal.

The 490 became Chevrolet's success story, establishing that auto maker as a trend setter in the low-price field. The model forever fashioned the direction of Chevrolet. Selling for $490 plus one option package at $60, which included electric lights and electric starter (two features not common to Model T Fords in the late teens), the 490 continued to be improved over the years and up to its last version in 1922. Durant used the profits and sales strength of the 490 Chevrolet to take over GM in 1918. Chevrolet's calendar year production grew in leaps. In its first production year, it was 2,999 units. In 1914 it came to 5,005. For 1915 it jumped to 13,292; for 1916 it hurtled to 62,898; and in 1917 reached 110,839. In 1922, the record stood at 208,848 and that figure would almost double for 1923.[2]

As good as the Chevrolet 490 was, it would not have been successful had there not been a winning field force to distribute the car. This included reputable and aggressive distributors, dealers, and sales staff.

Distributors often were set up by companies as direct representation points in key sales markets. In certain areas it made better sense to sell the distribution rights as a franchise to a local firm. The dealer system was then established within factory sanctioned borders, which usually covered a major portion of a state or several states. New cars were ordered by

The Chevrolet "490" was put on sale June 1, 1915, as a 1916 model. The hot-selling "490" became the cornerstone for William C. Durant's second automotive empire and leveraged him into command at General Motors for a second time.

dealers from the distributors, and distributors placed the orders with the factory. The system allowed for local character and heightened private interests.

Contracts between dealer and distributor as factory agents became the norm for the industry. Chevrolet used the system to its best. Even new cars needed to be serviced, and happy customers who had stayed in touch with a dealership for servicing often brought repeat business in new cars. The used car market blossomed in the 1920s, creating a new side business for dealers. William S. Knudsen, who had come from Ford, became president of Chevrolet in 1922 and continued the course toward success.

As early as 1916, in anticipation of historic sales achievements, Chevrolet officials made arrangements for dealers to get up to a 90 percent loan of the net billing price of new cars. This was a result of the company making "greater strides than any other automobile company in America."[3]

Large cities became focal points for the system of distribution. The sales dynamic was natural because where there are more people, there are more sales. But the shipping aspect was prominent, too. Most new cars went from factory to dealers

Not all dealers could afford large facilities. Many west of the Mississippi settled for smaller quarters. Buick, like other car makers, sought to strengthen its dealer network in the 1920s.

via railroad. Rail hubs were good sites for large distributor and dealer networks. While Henry Ford's dealer strength initially was geared toward the rural sector, Chevrolet's included strong outlets in big cities from the first.

Buick was taking on dealers in small towns in the 1920s. In Greenfield, Ill., South Side Hardware Company was named as an outlet in connection with the dealer in Carlinville. In Jacksonville, Ill., near the state capital, the Morgan County Motor Company was "hitting the ball hard" in sales. E. Lewis, Buick dealer in Marion, Ill., claimed that the 1925 season was the best ever.

Promotional stunts were used to gain the attention of the press. A Buick was used to promote Asheville, N.C., by the Chamber of Commerce in 1925. The Buick was taken on a 5,000 mile tour of about 35 major cities in the United States and Canada, and a list of 25,000 people were to receive personal calls. For servicing, the car stopped at Buick dealers. Dealers grabbed the opportunity to hype the event when the car came to their city, as a sign of the virtues of the Buick Standard Six.[4]

There was a changed outlook for the medium-price field in which Buick was entrenched as part of General Motors since

The first car used by the White House was a steamer. Among the great advances made in steam power was the Doble, made from 1914 to 1931. Unimpressed by the Stanley's factory, Abner Doble built his own steam car that recirculated steam for further use. Modern advances to his steam car kept it in news items before the public. Few were built, and charges of stock manipulation plus the Crash on Wall Street brought an end to the operation in April 1931.

Buick had established a solid network of distributors and dealers even before 1920. The reputation of the marque was not only based on reliability but on the service which these outlets offered for repairs and trade-ins.

1908. According to *Cram's Weekly Report to Automotive Clients*, dated August 7, 1925, one car maker "operating in two price classes ranging from $1,000 to $2,000 has set up a definite standard of values which should be continued through the year. Though too early to judge accurately, there are indications that the market for its product will be limited only by its ability to produce. This means that approximately 250,000 of the cars that will be sold in the next fiscal year (in this price range) will be produced by this one company. In a four-million-car year the car sales in this class would approximate 600,000, which would leave an approximate 350,000 cars for all other makers in this class. The combined production capacity in this price class is for about 1 million cars. . . . It appears certain that this one maker will hold its production volume despite competitive efforts. The effect of

In the early 1920s, concrete roads were few. Eight states each had more than 1,000 miles of concrete roads: New York, Pennsylvania, Ohio, Indiana, Michigan, Illinois, Wisconsin, and California. Three had between 500 and 1,000 miles: Maryland, North Carolina, and Washington. Ten had between 250 and 500: New Jersey, Virginia, West Virginia, Georgia, Minnesota, Iowa, Missouri, Kansas, Texas, and Arizona. States that had less than 100 miles included Maine, Vermont, New Hampshire, Rhode Island, Florida, Alabama, Tennessee, Kentucky, Louisiana, North and South Dakota, Nebraska, Montana, Wyoming, Idaho, and Nevada. The other states had between 100 and 250 miles of concrete roads. Congress had passed the Federal Aid Road Act in 1916 which appropriated $75 million to cooperate with states which chose to build rural post roads. Up to $20,000 per mile was given by the Federal government. By 1925 the amount appropriated over a nine year period was $615 million and by 1928 there were 184,000 miles of Federal Aid roads and 56,717 miles of highway. About 90 percent of the nation's population lived within 10 miles of these roads.[11]

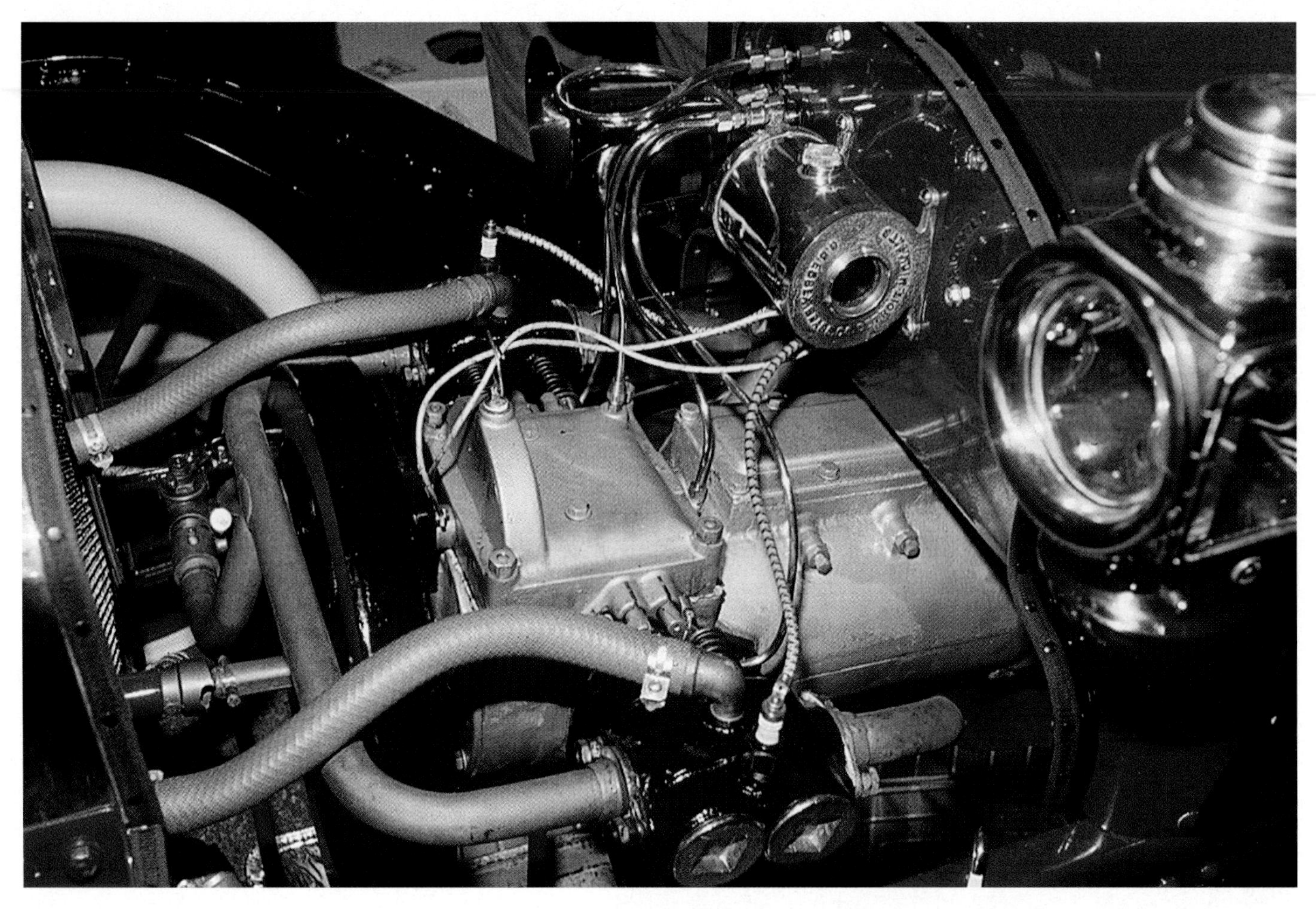

In the brass era before 1916, car engines predominated in two and four-cylinder form, hoods were easily removed, and simplicity of design prevailed, as on this Maxwell.

States were enacting laws that affected cars. In Illinois, "No red or green lights shall show in the direction (front) in which the vehicle is moving, except fire, police, and ambulance vehicles. Exhaust pipes must be parallel to the ground or directed slightly up, muffler cutouts operated from inside the car are prohibited, and gongs, bells, whistles, sirens (except on police cars, fire, and ambulance vehicles) are prohibited after Jan. 1, 1926."[12] As early as 1904, Michigan had legislated that all automobiles had to have two independent brakes. The first electric traffic signal was put in action in August of 1914 in Cleveland, Ohio.

the competition for the remaining business will be to force out those unable to hold paying volume."

Fierce competition and the control of parts sources had forced small manufacturers into red ink. The Gardner was one of the longest lived assembled cars, having been produced from 1920 to 1931. It was stylish and had a diverse distribution network with 75 distributors and just over 1,000 dealers. It was a well managed company that marked a profit until 1927. But competition was simply too strong.

In its 50th anniversary celebration of 1925-26 (the company, like Studebaker, had built buggies prior to cars), officials noted the wisdom of Thomas Edison: "Take away my organization and leave me my business and I am ruined. But take away my business and leave me my organization and I will soon be as big a factor as ever." The company began building new Chevrolet bodies alongside its wagons and by 1915 began the complete assembly of the car. Chevrolet production was controlled by the company up and down much of the Mississippi River. When family members entered military service in World War I, this Midwest Chevrolet business was sold to General Motors. After the war, the Gardner family made their own car. Management was so good at the company that it accounted for 10 percent of all

By the 1940s the straight eight engine had its days numbered. The V-8 was gaining in preference.

As styling advanced in the 1930s and as engines continued to grow in displacement, engine compartments became crowded, as on this Cord.

On January 6, 1925, a silver anniversary celebration for the American automobile industry was held by the National Automobile Chamber of Commerce. The year 1900 was chosen as the beginning of the industry, and 11 living pioneers were honored with large silver medals at a special dinner: John D, Maxwell, Edgar L. Apperson, A. L. Riker, John S. Clarke, Rollin H. White, H. H. Franklin, Charles Duryea, Charles B. King, Elwood Haynes, Alexander Winton, and R. E. Olds.[13]

American-made cars sent to South America and had dealers in 26 countries. But in the late 1920s management saw how the future of the car business was questionable for a small company.[5]

Franklin, advertised as the air-cooled favorite of famous aviators, had a strong dealer network in the 1920s. *Dealers' Bulletin* was a newsletter that told of dealer successes and company achievements. For the first two weeks in August 1928 sales were up by 54 percent over the similar period in 1926. One dealer reported that these makes were being traded toward new Franklins: two 1927 Packards, a 1928 Marmon, a 1927 Cadillac, a 1927 Studebaker President, a 1925 Jordan, and a 1923 Studebaker. Franklin was claiming 25 percent of the fine car business that month. One senator purchased his 37th Franklin by telephone in August 1928, and while Franklin sales against water-cooled cars were good in Chicago, Milwaukee, Kansas

The Evolution of Fender Design

Hardly more than mud shields, fenders before 1905 were functional and certainly not decorative.

By the early 1920s fenders had become rounded and offered a styling statement besides remaining practical.

By 1933 skirts along the lower portion of fenders predicted the partial enveloping of wheels. Side mounted spare tires often were nestled into fenders on large and expensive cars, although the option could be had on low priced cars if clearance for the front door allowed it.

By 1937, front fenders covered most of the tire and wheel. The advantages for future streamlining against wind resistance were readily accepted by many engineers and stylists. (Photo by M. Lawrence Hassel)

The dashboard of the 1937 Cord reflected the industry's move toward jewel-like details blended with eye-pleasing balance and motoring practicality. (Photo by M. Lawrence Hassel)

City, Denver, and Columbus, it was still eastern cities in states such as Pennsylvania and New York that brought ongoing sales success to the make. But the days of regional sales strengths to carry a company toward stronger and stronger growth were numbered. Franklin was to have its greatest days in the 1920s; 1934 models would mark its conclusion as the last of the early major auto makers to offer air-cooled engines.

No longer would the American automotive scene offer a wide range of makes as previously. By the close of the decade the large number of medium-priced contenders had been whittled to Auburn, Buick, Chrysler, Dodge, Durant, Graham, Hudson, Hupmobile, Jordan, Nash, Oakland, Oldsmobile, Reo, Studebaker, and Willys-Knight, and entering this field in 1926 was Peerless and in 1927, Marmon.[6] William C. Durant launched his final automotive empire by purchasing Locomobile and Mason in 1922. In 1927 he planned to combine Star, Moon, Chandler, Gardner, Hupmobile, Jordan, and Peerless, but it did not materialize.

The survival rate for car makers across all price classes was grimmer yet. From 1903 to 1926, forty-nine companies had lasted only one to three years; forty had lasted four to six years; and twenty-six had made it to their seventh to ninth year. Eighteen had lasted from ten to twelve years. Only seventeen

By 1930, the export of American-made cars had resulted in some lavish distributor and dealer operations overseas, such as this one for Packard in Melbourne, Australia.

had lasted twenty-two years or more in business. The rate of failure in the first three years was 28 percent. Based upon statistics of other branches of manufacturing, the rate of failure among car companies was high.

In 1926 94.1 percent of dealers surveyed reported a profit, while only 3.5 percent had a loss. The rest broke even. In 1927 the figures were 86.6 percent with a profit, 8.6 percent with a loss. In 1929 that slipped to 75.1 percent at profit, 15.5 percent at loss. The new car market was changing, and the auto makers plus their distributors and dealers were obliged to keep up with the times.[7]

The automobile had changed America by 1929. Social, civic, and educational activities—even religious endeavors—in the rural landscape had become fashioned by the automobile. Farm families were linked more closely with towns. Buses transported children to school and churches became bigger due to the mobility of their parishioners. Many businesses simply got bigger due to widened markets. "To many the automobile furnished an extraordinary incentive to work—hence became a prime factor in creating for the masses standards of living never before thought possible."[8] Good roads were in demand; suburbs formed around large cities; emergency vehicles carried the ill to

The nearly complete line of Packards was displayed at the Melbourne location, which helped to boost sales of the luxury marque along with its international reputation. Other makes were following suit.

the hospital; motorized hearses carried citizens to their final rest. "The automobile made touring a national pastime. In 1930 the United States Forest Service reported that more than 29,500,000 visitors to the national forests traveled by automobile," which amounted to 92.6 of all visitors![9] Each year as many as 40 million Americans took to the roads for vacations in the late 1920s.

While the automobile industry was here to stay, many of its players were to face hard times ahead. The formula for success and survival would depend on all five elements—especially the element of meeting the needs of the public. And for this, styling and pricing were to play major roles.

Notes

1. Chevrolet dealer letter issued by the Kansas City distributor, July 12, 1917.

2. *The Production Figure Book for U.S. Cars*, Jerry Heasley, Motorbooks International, Osceola, Wis., 1977; page 117.

3. Chevrolet dealer letter issued by Kansas City distributor, November 24, 1916; dealers obtained their loan through the American Commercial Company, Cleveland, Ohio. The move was meant to build up substantial stocks among dealers during winter months, thus keeping the factory operational and putting the burden for sales success upon the dealers. Henry Ford had followed his own techniques in unburdening the factory when sales seemed to slow and the dealers either accepted the financial obligation or lost their connection with Ford.

4. These and other dealer-related facts in this section come from the *Vesper-Buick Bulletin* issued by a prominent Midwest Buick distributor in the mid-1920s.

5. From Gardner, a prestige portfolio issued by the company to its dealers as "sales policies and advertising plans for 1925-26," courtesy C. E. Thomas. Helpful comments also from the *Standard Catalog of American Cars, 1805-1942*, Kimes & Clark, Krause Publications, Iola, Wis., 1985; page 571.

6. *The Passenger Car Industry, Report of a Survey*, Charles Coolidge Parlin and Fred Bremier, The Curtis Publishing Co., Philadelphia, 1932; page 31. This survey was done nationwide and is compared to a similar study done in 1914.

7. Ibid., page 62. Comments about survival rates are based on *The Automobile Industry*. . . , Epstein, pp. 163, 164, 168, and 347.

8. Ibid,, pp. 11, 12.

9. Ibid.

10. *American Automobile Digest*, W. L. Gordon, editor, Cincinnati, Ohio, August 1923; page 64.

11. Ibid., p. 28, and *The Automobile Industry*. . . , Epstein.

12. Bulletin No. 2041, Vesper-Buick Auto Co., August 4, 1925.

13. *The Automobile Industry*. . . , Epstein; a flyleaf photo of the awardees with caption give the details.

The Leland-built Lincoln proudly announced its lineage on its radiator badge. After engineering the Cadillac, Henry Leland went on to make the Lincoln in 1920. Before Leland's efforts, five other companies had either planned to sell cars under the Lincoln name or actually produced a modest amount of Lincoln cars, altogether different than the Leland version.

Saxons were made in Detroit and, later, in Ypsilanti, Mich. The Saxon Motor Company was headed by Harry Ford, whose similarity in name to Henry Ford was hoped to be a sales advantage. The Saxon was made from 1913 to 1922 and initially sold for only $395.

From 1905 to 1929 the Moon motor car was one of the more successful Midwestern automobiles made outside of Detroit. In 1928 production reached 3,000. In its late years, the car sported a Rolls-Royce "look-alike" radiator design.

With an influx of Cadillac executives and fueled by the energies of Charles W. Nash, the LaFayette debuted for 1921. But in 1924, the last models were made. The car was separate from the Nash operation. Although talks took place toward a merger of LaFayette and Pierce-Arrow, little transpired.

Minnesota's most distinguished motor car was the Luverne, made from 1904 to 1916. Model Fifty, the Montana Special, gained its fame in the Big Sky country as early as 1913. The company also made fire engines and trucks.

The Moline had a 40 hp engine with a bore and stroke of 4 ⅛th by 6 inches, claimed to be "The Longest Stroke Motor Made in America." The car was made from 1904 to 1913 and was followed by the Moline-Knight from 1914 to 1919.

Seven different brands of cars carried the Monarch name from Aurora and Chicago Heights, Ill., Milwaukee, Wis., New York, N.Y., Cleveland, Ohio, and Detroit, Mich. The most successful seems to be the last, which was in production from 1913 to 1916. Joseph Bloom, company organizer, had another car connection. His brother-in-law was Robert C. Hupp.

Easily converted from a car to light truck was the Chase, made from 1907 to 1912 in Syracuse, N.Y. It was a highwheeler with chain drive and solid rubber tires. The Chase Motor Truck Company was the manufacturer.

Chapter 5

Rebounding from Near Disaster

The 1929 Buick still catered to its family-oriented clientele with conservative colors, especially on closed cars. The rear-mounted spare tire was a common sight by 1930 and visually lengthened the car.

The convertible victoria was a refined body style for the majestic Duesenberg of the early 1930s.

For 1936 Auburn offered 36 body styles among seven model designations ranging from Standard to Supercharged Dual Ratio. Prices ran from $745 to $2,245.

"I have maintained all through the depression that this country had great latent purchasing power. Plymouth and Dodge sales have proved it. Recently this buying power has become more active under the stimulus of returning confidence. That activity is now creating more employment and in turn producing more purchasing power. I believe that is how we are going to get

Chrysler's Imperial for 1933 was a regal platform for custom coachwork. In the doldrums of the Great Depression, it was still fashionable for the wealthy who had retained their standing to order special-bodied cars befitting their status. However, some wealthy buyers chose not to flaunt their wealth in order to avoid public attention, which at times turned into near-riots when a fancy car wandered into the wrong neighborhood.

Packard still presided over the luxury car field as a volume producer of fine cars. Even this Standard Eight, an all-weather cabriolet (town car) version, dictated luxury. LeBaron bodies could be ordered from factory catalogs, and other houses of custom design—a throwback to the carriage trade—also liked the Packard chassis.

on our way in this country. The greatest thing that President Roosevelt has done is to give people the spark of confidence to start things going again." So said Walter P. Chrysler, board chairman of the corporation that carried his name. His words were directed to Chrysler dealers in a special communiqué dated

The radio industry benefited from the growth of the auto industry in the 1930s. Buyers were fascinated by the rise of radio in the late 1920s, so it was only a matter of time before the radio could be adapted for automobile use. In a special sales promotion kit, dealers of the Delco Auto Radio were told in 1936: "There is an almost unbelievable market for Auto Radio. There are 23 million motor cars in operation in the United States today and only 4.5 million of these are radio equipped. Think of it—[an] 18.5 million car market on which to work. . . . Radio is only 16 years old, and in that time has become one of America's greatest industries." Only 3,000 sets were in use in cars for 1929. This grew to 1.1 million for 1935. The Delco Auto Radio was made for Chevrolet, Pontiac, Oldsmobile, Buick, Ford and Lincoln Zephyr, Plymouth, Hudson and Terraplane, and Dodge. Prices ranged from $39.95 to $69.95. In 1936, the rubberized Flex-O-Strip antenna, mounted under running boards, was listed at $5.50 in universal type.

Body by Fisher
Possession ···MAKES THE HEART BEAT FASTER··

Buick
BUICK this year is widening the tremendous favor it holds with people who live in the modern manner. Its beauty, its luxury, its quiet sophistication, are in their language, as its sturdy dependability and mighty performance are in the universal language of motoring.
Buick engineering creates a different and finer kind of motoring—the Buick kind. It adapts Knee-Action wheels to Buick's own requirements for the gliding ride. But it doesn't stop there. It goes all the way to the gliding ride as only Buick gives it. It builds in a new balance of weight and springing, and a new ride stabilizer; it equips with new air-cushion tires. Then it provides center-point steering for your greater surety of control; vacuum-power brakes for your greater safety; automatic starting and other operations for your greater convenience and ease, and your car's increased efficiency.
In less than an hour you can learn why Buick is cresting the flood of popularity—and discover that just the thought of possessing it for your own makes your heart beat faster.
· BUICK ·
WHEN · BETTER · AUTOMOBILES · ARE · BUILT — BUICK · WILL · BUILD · THEM

By the mid-1930s Buicks made "the heart beat faster," ad writers contended. Most of America was introduced to new cars in the 1930s through ads appearing in national magazines. There was no commercial television to hype the models, and it was hard to explain how a new car looked over the radio!

May 25, 1933. Had he known how difficult future years in that decade would be, he might not have spoken so optimistically.

The economic Crash of Wall Street had ushered in the worst depression to hit the United States. Because for many people an automobile was the second most costly purchase outside of a house, sales were an early casualty. Many people opted to buy food and clothing and keep a roof above head rather than own a new car. As the jobless rate rose, the sales of new cars and even their maintenance by dealers plummeted.

It was a combination of circumstances that moved the auto industry to advance its sales based on styling in the 1930s. Streamlining was a natural direction as cars became mechanically refined. And styling, it was hoped, would garner

Cadillac had established itself as a rising star among luxury cars by 1930. Besides V-8 versions, the GM division took pride in offering V-16 and V-12 versions in the 1930s, just the thing for the ultra wealthy to order with a custom body.

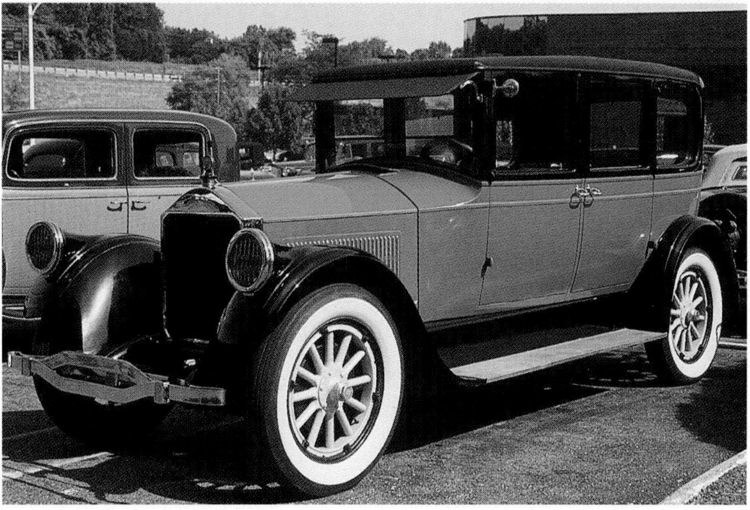

In the mid-1920s, Pierce-Arrow styling reflected the boxy design typical of the decade. While an innovative predictor of headlights built into the fenders, the company's conservative bend would fail to save the company during the economic upheaval of the 1930s. (Photo by M. Lawrence Hassel)

more attention from the public and result in increased sales. Styling emphasis was not only applied to the exterior as fenders enveloped wheels, roof lines were rounded, and lower silhouettes

The proud heritage of Marmon ended with production of 1933 models. The company had begun production in 1902 in Indianapolis and was respected in the luxury class. It had grown from a one-room cabin with a single forge to a complex covering 67 acres. The Nordyke & Marmon Company had begun in 1851 with the manufacture of flour milling machinery. The name was of French origin, a derivation of Marmont. In literature issued in 1928, the company noted the loyalty of Marmon owners: "A garage burned to the ground; 25 Marmons were burned; 25 Marmon owners had the opportunity of buying any car on the market; 25 of them bought Marmons." The company claimed to have produced the first V-type engine as early as 1904. Out of 113 races entered in 1909, Marmons won first place 35 times; second place, 30 times; and third place, 20 times. It was the Marmon Wasp with Ray Harroun at the wheel that won the first 500 Mile Sweepstakes Race at the Indianapolis Motor Speedway "against the best that America and Europe had to offer, and came into international fame."

Buick aimed for the young at heart with its spring-like ad campaign for 1928. Colorful expressions had once more gained the upper hand in the auto industry.

were revealed. Interior appointments were part of the styling advance, since an owner spent more time inside the car than looking at it from afar. To impress the neighbors, exterior appearances were important; to impress the owner, nicely appointed interiors were crucial. Nash, taking this a step further in 1938, developed its conditioned air system for interior comfort, taking fresh air, filtering it, heating it, and circulating it for maximum effect.

Of all decades in the industry's first 100 years, the 1930s likely mark the greatest changes in styling and mechanical innovations. A car from 1930 looks vastly antiquated when compared to an offering from 1939. And among all marques of the decade, there were three prime examples of early styling experiments: Graham, Pierce-Arrow, and Chrysler.

For Graham and Pierce-Arrow, survival was at stake. With its 1930 production being only 33,560, Graham was at less than half of 1929 production. For 1931, it fell to 20,428. A bold stroke

While not a classic car according to historic standards, Pontiac for 1936 was a good car ranging in price from $615 to $855. Its "waterfall" grille was new this year and the styling motif would stick with Pontiac into the 1950s.

For 1940, Pontiac emerged as a lower, more streamlined and refined version of its 1936 counterpart.

Cord, the last of the Auburn, Ind., trio from the classic period, found its final expression in the ageless "coffin-nose" beauty of 1936 and 1937.

For Those Who Know and Appreciate the Finest in Motor Cars
CHRYSLER has wrought in the 112 h.p. Imperial "80" an entirely new kind of performance, style and appearance in the field of the finest cars . . . ¶ Its engine is unmatched for smooth power. It has an extraordinary reserve to achieve further marvels in speed, acceleration and hill-climbing . . . ¶ Its bodies are remarkable for their long, graceful lines, their fine upholstery and fittings, charm and diversity of chromatic colorings, and are indeed luxurious without even a hint of over-ornamentation . . . ¶ Ownership of a Chrysler Imperial "80" indicates appreciation of the finest in motor cars.
THE NEW 112 H.P.
CHRYSLER
IMPERIAL "80"
Roadster (with rumble seat), $2795; Five-Passenger Sedan, $2945; Town Sedan, $2995; Seven-Passenger Sedan, $3075; Sedan-Limousine, $3495; also in custom-built types by Dietrich, LeBaron and Locke. All prices f. o. b. Detroit, subject to current Federal excise tax.

Chrysler showed colorful creativity in its promotional campaigns during the classic era. The boxy form of the American car was epitomized in the Imperial "80," for 1928.

of styling debuted for 1932: the Blue Streak Eight, a daring design that made the small auto maker a pacesetter. A veed and slanted grille covered the radiator, fenders were curvaceous and skirted, and the general appearance was modern. It was a lot of styling savvy for just over $1,000. Trouble was, fewer and fewer people had that much money to spend on a new car. Sales were affected and Graham placed 17th in the industry, with 8,001 cars for 1932. While that was a slight rise from its 19th place for 1931, it was hardly worth cheering.[1]

In the early 1930s, a legend was nearing its end. Pierce-Arrow was hard hit by the Depression as the luxury class of cars faced an evaporating pool of buyers. The make took 25th place in sales for 1930 with only 6,795 cars. For 1931 it took 22nd place with 4,522. It held that place for 1933, but sales dipped to an appalling 2,481 vehicles. Conservative styling was a hallmark of luxury cars. Owners who put up $5,000 for a new car in the early 1930s could have bought a nice house for the same money; they did not want styling that obviously went out of date in a year or two. But conservative styling wasn't selling Pierce-Arrows like it had.

The V-12 Silver Arrow of 1933 offered hope. Front fender lines swept rearward, uninterrupted. Rear wheels were skirted almost completely from view. The roof line was rakish. The body

The 1937 Chrysler Airflow was the last of its breed. The Airflow experiment had cost the Chrysler Corporation millions of dollars due to a generally negative public reaction in sales. However, the Airflow remains one of the shining lights in the history of aerodynamic design and safety construction.

was tapered at the rear for a sporty look. With this styling and selling for $10,000, it was a publicity magnet for the press. But only six Silver Arrows were made. The experiment did not magically rub off on other models in the Pierce-Arrow line up. New car registrations continued their hopeless descent: 1934—1,740; 1935—875; 1936—787; 1937—167; and 1938—less than 100.[2]

Bravery often is slow when it comes to launching a new design into unknown sales waters. General Motors had experimented with companion cars to its main makes in 1929: the Viking V-8 by Oldsmobile and the Buick Marquette. Both became fast casualties. GM was to launch many of its cautious styling advances in 1934 and 1935 and like other auto makers was promoting independent front suspension as a great step forward in steering and comfortable ride. Ford, Hupmobile, and others were equally cautious. Studebaker introduced Free Wheeling in 1930. The feature was a flop. Terror stories circulated, involving mountainous terrain that allowed Studebakers with Free Wheeling to accelerate to dangerous speeds without the engine or transmission to brake the action. In regards to styling, Studebaker was only mildly innovative. Some

Franklin had given up its horse collar design on its simulated radiator in 1924. For 1925 and 1926 the make carried a conventional style for its dummy radiator. The classic period of styling had come to the American automobile and Franklin reflected the times. In 1933 and 1934, the last years for the make, a V-12 was offered in four body styles and sold for as much as $4,185. (Photo by M. Lawrence Hassel)

Chrysler Airflow production was concentrated in the four-door sedan. For the CU Series in 1934 there were 7,226 four-door sedans; 732 rumble seat coupes; 306 two-door sedans; and 125 town sedans; total production for the Chrysler Airflow that year came to 8,389. In Imperial form, Series CV, there were 1,997 four door sedans, 212 five passenger sedans, and 67 town sedans. The Imperial Series CX had 78 limousines lead its total production of 106, and in the CX# Custom Imperial line, 20 limousines and two-town limousines were manufactured. The Imperial Airflow Series CY saw 399 four door sedans, 37 rumble seat coupes, and nine two door sedans. For 1935 Chrysler Airstream production came to 24,458 vs. only 2,598 Airflows. Imperial Airstream production was 9,297 vs. 5,200 for all Imperial Airflows. Evidently the luxury car buyer was more willing to experiment with the Airflow than was the buyer of medium priced cars![9]

bold moves were short lived, such as the Cord with coffin-nose design for 1936 and 1937. But officials at Chrysler were enjoying grand sales successes for a young corporation and, when it came to design, were ready for a giant step into the future.

The Airflow resulted.

It was a design that was built for safety, was aerodynamic, and looked ultra modern. The work was exploratory and exploded typical reasoning held by designers, recalled Carl Breer, one of Chrysler's main engineers. It was the first serious result of air tunnel testing. The rear seat was moved forward about 20 inches to cradle the passengers and allow for a bulbous design that was in keeping with "nature's fundamental laws." What resulted was a lower center of gravity and superior roadability, better springing, better overall balance, and increased stability. The monocoque (vehicle construction in which the body is integral with the chassis) all-steel body was innovative and predicted the industry's future. More interior room and comforts made the car luxurious and pointed to the trend of medium and low priced cars claiming features that had been reserved for high priced makes.[3] In styling and engineering, it was an innovation. When the car buyer of 1933 stood next to an Airflow, he or she must have felt as if the car had just landed from outer space. For some buyers this was intriguing. For others, it looked like a scary investment.

So it is with innovation. Early in the century President Teddy Roosevelt had claimed that a man should be just slightly ahead of his time, otherwise he walks too far ahead of the people. Evidently such wisdom was not followed by officials at Chrysler when the Airflow bowed.

Difficulties resulted. The corporation had swung the weight of its Chrysler and DeSoto production toward the Airflow design in a major commitment amid a depression. While Walter P. Chrysler and industry analysts were predicting a return to normalcy for the car market in the mid 1930s, it was not to be: 1938 was another severe year for sales and it would take defense contracts preliminary to World War II to help lift the economic burden of the automotive industry.

The formula for success was at risk. Meeting the needs of the public would equate to good sales, but Chrysler was facing a dilemma. The American Manufacturers Association was reporting that 95 percent of all cars were selling for less than $750 wholesale. The Chrysler and DeSoto Airflows were considerably above this figure, the less costly DeSoto version for 1934 selling at a base price of $995. The corporation had poured many millions of dollars into the Airflow with no apparent Plan B in case sales were poor. While a very good car, it became known as the turkey that threatened corporate success. The Airstream design—a rehashing of typical styling—was offered alongside the Airflow, while the Airflow agonized in sales toward its discontinuation at the end of the 1937 model year.

What buoyed the corporation during the Airflow was the profit from Dodge and especially Plymouth. To gear for good sales, officials at Chrysler told the dealer network in 1933 that "we understand. . . many dealers of our competitors are planning to dispense with a great many retail salesmen in the near future. If this is done, a wonderful opportunity will be presented to enlist many able salesmen into Chrysler ranks."[4] Mr. Chrysler pushed his dealers, who were not keeping enough new cars in showrooms. He told all district and branch managers, "Your district men should be advised of this and get their noses wiped as this matter is going to be taken up every 90 days. The Sales Divisions are going to be held responsible for not having their territories in first class shape."[5] Joseph W. Frazer, then general sales manager, told his field force, "I am not at all pleased with the volume of business that we are getting on Plymouth." While allotments of Chryslers were on target, Plymouths had slipped

Compared to styling yet to come, many cars were stodgy dressers against the likes of the 1942 Lincoln Zephyr. The Zephyr bowed for 1936 in "teardrop" form. By the early 1940s that design would sacrifice aerodynamics for the stately look of the Continental.

With the encouragement of Charles Kettering, General Motors turned its attention to diesel engines during the Great Depression. On a design drafted by Kettering, the corporation moved into new territory. In 1930 it absorbed the Winton Engine Company of Cleveland and the Electro-Motive Corporation, which made railroad equipment powered by internal combustion engines and electric drive. Diversification would become an even greater catalyst for the formula of success in future years.[10]

The 1936 Ford in tudor version brought sporty looks to the low-price class during the classic era. Edsel Ford was now head of the company, but his father, Henry, was prone to second-guessing his son.

below expectation, although the company publicly took pride in great sales achievements. "We have about 11,000 Plymouth orders on our books for August (1933) shipment; we should have at least 17,000. This division is perfectly capable of selling 20,000 Plymouths in a month like this, but as it is, we will ship only about 12,000."[6]

However, while brands of cars made by other companies were slipping in sales, Plymouth was gaining. Problem was, the corporation expected bigger gains. Those profits fed the Airflow.

Ford officials watched the aerodynamic advance of the Airflow but launched its streamlined car amid caution. The 1936 Lincoln-Zephyr was a sleek-styled 12-cylinder foray into the medium-price class. Handsome in the eyes of many buyers, the car still carried its Ford heritage in looks, especially for fenders, hood, and grille. More than 15,000 were made that first year. But by 1938 and 1939, sales seemed to level around 20,000.

The addition of Mercury for 1939 was to fill a price gap in the Ford family of fine cars, but the car was a glorified Ford more than a downsized Lincoln. Caution ruled. The aggressiveness of Chrysler leadership, even though the

Packard for 1938 was still sticking to its noble V-12 engine, which the company claimed was the best balanced design for a motor. The Packard V-12 would wave farewell in 1939. However, it was the straight eight engine that brought good sales to the luxury marque and proved to be a very reliable power plant with lots of performance.

corporation was at about 40 percent of its production capacity in the Depression, helped move the auto maker into second place behind General Motors, and Ford slipped to third—a position that lasted from 1933 to 1950.[7]

Others in the industry watched the Airflow experiment. A radically new design could be a catalyst in the formula for success. Charles F. Kettering, vice president for General Motors, noted in 1939, "What will we manufacture when our present products are obsolete? What change will the future bring that will affect our way of thinking or of doing things? As the days, seasons, and years pass, will we have the increment of change ready which (buyers) are sure to demand? And we know they will demand change for that has been our experience every day of our life since we were born. Maybe we could learn something from the dressmakers who change styles with every season. They carry over very little from the past and obsolete their product four times a year.

In March of 1933 Studebaker went into receivership and soon after President Albert Erskine committed suicide. But the company was successful during the lean years of the 1930s due to worthy management of Harold Vance and Paul Hoffman. In mid-1939 the Champion series, seen here in its basically unchanged version for 1940, was introduced. With the help of the popular Champion, model year production for 1939 was up to 85,834, which was a considerable rise over the 1938 level of 46,787.

"Industry must do one great thing. It must recognize that out of the laboratories new industries are born. For years we have been using the scientific information in making our products which was discovered over 50 years ago. Now we very badly need new fundamental information from which to create new job making industries.

"We have only started. There are more things to be done than at any time in our history. I'd like to start a library some day. Our present libraries contain the records of everything that is known. I want to build one to hold the books on everything we don't know."[8]

Notes

1. *Standard Catalog of American Cars, 1805-1942*, Kimes & Clark, Krause Publications, Iola, Wis., 1985; and *Encyclopedia of American Cars 1930 to 1942*, James H. Moloney, edited by George H. Dammann, Crestline Publishing, Glen Ellyn, Ill., 1977; see appropriate entries by make. In 1934 officials of Graham-Paige met with counterparts for Reo and Hupmobile to explore a merger. However, Hupp officials balked at the proposals, killing the plan.

2. Ibid.

3. *The Birth of Chrysler Corporation and Its Engineering Legacy*, Carl Breer, edited by Anthony J. Yanik, Society of Automotive Engineers, Warrendale, Pa., 1995; pp. 166 & 167. The book is historically significant in its indepth overview of the Airflow.

4. Corporate letter from director of sales, Chrysler Sales Corporation, for November 7, 1933.

5. Inter-company correspondence, August 17, 1933.

6. Ibid.

7. *The American Automobile*, John B. Rae, University of Chicago Press, Chicago, 1965; p. 117.

8. *Automobile Book of the Year 1939, An Age of Wheelprints*, issued for the Chicago Automobile Show, November 12-19, 1938, by the Chicago Automobile Trade Association. Kettering's comments appear to have been a speech to dealers and industry leaders. Kettering is credited with advancing the use of the automobile by perfecting the electric starter in 1912.

9. Figures based on *The Production Figure Book for U.S. Cars* by Heasley.

10. Ibid., *The American Automobile*, p. 118.

Stutz, a proud maker of luxury cars built on a reputation of performance and safety, began production in 1911. Its final offerings bade farewell in 1934, with just six cars being made, a casualty of the Depression. In the 1930s fewer than 1,000 cars were produced.

Hupmobile tried valiantly to survive the economic unrest of the decade. Its eight cylinder engine first appeared for 1925, when sales and hopes were strong. For 1934 the maker offered seven series and a total of 26 body styles. For 1939 that dwindled to three series and six body styles.

The American Austin was made in Butler, Pa., from 1930 to 1934. It was a classy looking diminutive car, hardly comfortable for two passengers. The design was by Alexis de Saknoffsky. Compared to the next smallest car in the land, the Austin was 16 inches narrower and 28 inches shorter. It s initial factory price was $445 in roadster form.

In the early to mid-1920s the "dogbone" motometer, a radiator temperature gauge, was common fare for the front of almost any new car. But the day of practicality was to end soon. (Photo by M. Lawrence Hassel)

By the late 1920s, luxury cars were going one better by adding special touches to the heat gauge up front, as seen on this 1926 Packard. The flying goddess or "doughnut pusher" symbol would be carried on Packard hood ornaments through the 1950 model. (Photo by M. Lawrence Hassel)

This 1932 Studebaker hood ornament shows the streamlined art-deco taste of the times. Gone is the heat gauge, relegated to the dash. The ornament had become a decorative expression of the auto makers and would remain so well into the 1950s.

© 1945 The Studebaker Corporation

It's a jungle "Weasel" too!

STUDEBAKER'S amazing new Weasel personnel and cargo carrier is now in action in the Pacific islands—advancing, as it has been doing in Europe, over terrain that seems impossible for any mechanized military vehicle to negotiate.

The Weasel glides forward swiftly and stealthily in mud and swamp as well as on sand and snow—floats like a boat in lakes and rivers, as its powerful Studebaker Champion engine propels it from shore to shore.

This new "Champion" in invasion warfare not only transports men and supplies but also serves to carry wounded back to hospital areas. It's geared to clamber up seemingly impossible grades on its flexible, rubber-padded tracks.

Built by Studebaker, powered by the famous Studebaker Champion engine, the Weasel supplements such other Studebaker war production assignments as Wright Cyclone engines for the Boeing Flying Fortress and heavy-duty military trucks.

Awarded To All *Studebaker Plants*

Studebaker PIONEER AND PACEMAKER IN AUTOMOTIVE PROGRESS

Now building Wright Cyclone engines for the Boeing Flying Fortress — heavy-duty Studebaker military trucks—the Army's versatile personnel and cargo carrier, the Weasel.

YOUR WAR BONDS HELP KEEP THE FLYING FORTRESSES FLYING

Keep on buying War Bonds and keep the War Bonds you buy. They're the world's best investment. Every $3 you put up comes back to you worth $4.

Chapter 6

In Defense of Freedom and the Resulting New Order

By 1940 many of America's automotive pioneers and early corporate big wheels had passed. Death had called Albert Pope in 1909, John M. Studebaker in 1917, Francis E. Stanley in 1918, John and Horace Dodge plus Elmer Apperson in 1920, William Doud Packard in 1923, Elwood Haynes in 1925, and in 1928 James Ward Packard and Jonathan D. Maxwell. David Dunbar Buick died in 1929 and Harry C. Stutz in 1930. An especially bad year was 1932, which claimed Henry Leland, Alexander Winton, Hugh Chalmers, Fred Duesenberg, Roy A. Graham, and George B. Selden. John Willys North passed in 1933. Fred O. Paige died in 1935 and Roy D. Chapin followed in 1936. In 1940 Walter P. Chrysler passed away. Other pioneers still lived; but the class was dwindling.

Yet, their contributions to the advance of motoring in America had brought the industry to world domination. No other nation had so strong and diverse an automotive industry, and this fact was to play a major role in World War II.

The five elements in the formula of success remained crucial: (1) The source of motive power was still the internal combustion gasoline engine; (2) Mass production techniques were being refined year after year; (3) Precision manufacturing seemed to be ever on the increase; (4) Good distribution systems through distributors and dealers were being improved whenever possible;

Studebaker was a major producer of war goods, especially trucks and the Weasel, shown here. Ad campaigns were used by the industry to salve the car-buying desires of the public and to show how car makers were joining in the defense of the nation.

Chrysler, Buick, and Cadillac were leaders among makers of heavy battle equipment, such as the trustworthy and nimble Sherman tank, which was produced in such great numbers that the Axis Powers, though fielding better tanks, could not stem the tide of victory.

and (5) Meeting the needs of the public was foremost in the vision of corporate planners. Soon these five elements were to be applied in ways and on a scale that the auto industry had never done before.

Clouds of war approached America in 1940. Nazi Germany and Fascist Italy had proved their warlike tendencies in Africa and Europe. Imperial Japan was run by warlords who had eliminated or neutralized other world powers from their sphere of influence, with the exception of the United States. Defensive preparedness was an increasing theme in American society.

When new cars for 1940 were introduced in late 1939, there was great hope that sales were on the rebound from the Great Depression. The auto industry had been reshaped by the financial disaster and its aftermath. Lost in the economic conflagration were some favored marques: Auburn, Cord, Duesenberg, Moon (which was plagued by corporate intrigue even before the Crash of Wall Street), Kissel, Pierce-Arrow,

Packard held on to its older style for 1941 and on convertibles and certain high-priced offerings in 1942. The conservative car maker had repositioned itself amid the changed market that emerged from the Great Depression, now aiming as a volume builder of medium-price vehicles. This "120" eight-passenger station wagon sold new for $1,541 in Deluxe form. In comparison, a Chevrolet station wagon for 1941 sold at $995.

Peerless, LaFayette by Nash, Cunningham, du Pont, Durant, Elcar, Essex, Franklin, Gardner, Marmon, Reo (which moved into truck production), Stearns-Knight, Stutz, and Whippet. Hupmobile was breathing its last breath with the resurrected Cord body, and Graham wasn't too far behind with the same style. LaSalle was to be seen in its final form in 1940 as Cadillac downscaled its line to absorb that portion of the sales market. Ten years after the Crash, the market was vastly different. In 1940 the remaining car makers took aim at increased market shares due to the thinning of the ranks.

In April 1941 Oldsmobile produced confidential data on its dealer operation for 1939 and 1940. Statistics show how this division of General Motors had recovered. In 1939 there were 593 Oldsmobile dealers listed in the study. They sold 79,054 new Oldsmobiles and 10,039 of other makes. Total retail sales came to $81,116,787. For 1940 there were 602 dealers selling 110,327 Oldsmobiles and 10,343 of other makes bringing in $113,284,412 in retail sales. Used car sales had risen from just under $55 million in 1939 to over $68.3 million for 1940. Total

Lincoln carried its prewar design with trim updates through 1948. From 1949 through 1951, sleeker styling resulted. Some company executives did not appreciate the sad-looking frontal treatment with frenched headlights and longed for the return of the classic look. Mercury was upgraded in 1949 to look more like a Lincoln than a Ford.

One major oil company reported that service items such as tires, batteries, fan belts, spark plugs, and the like brought sales of $500 million for 1948 and were on the increase. Permanent anti-freeze was still gaining in popularity against the glycerine and alcohol mixture that boiled away. Tire chains were a must for driving in snow, and improved versions had flattened links where the chain met the tread to preserve the life of tires. Plastic-coated natural fibers were weaved into seat covers as a popular option in the 1940s. They were available at dealers and local service stations.[7]

car profit per dealer came to $115,000 in 1939 and $113,000 for 1940. Overhead had cut into profits, but the future was looking good. By the end of August 1941 there were 754 dealers in the Oldsmobile camp and 99.2 percent of those were turning a profit, up from 91.7 percent for 1940. Service gross profit, however, was rated nationally just below the "good" range.

Certain options were being pushed for the highest profit possible. Hydramatic sold for $95 but brought the dealer a gross profit of $22.80. The Master Radio option sold for $65.50 and resulted in a dealer gross profit of $30.70. Rear fender panels sold for $14 and brought a dealer profit of $4.80. At the low end of profits were such items as a horizontal grille bar, which sold for $4.25 ($1.70 profit), and plastic radiator ornament, which sold for $3 ($1.20 profit). By the beginning of the 1940s, dealers were contacting 35 prospective buyers and selling one car as a result of these contacts.[1]

Cars for 1940 generally carried brighter interiors. Hudson and Chrysler indulged in colors and combinations like never before. Plastic, which was a costly material to use in automobile production in 1940, was applied to the dashes of higher priced models in various makes, even on conservative Packard. The plastic molded to intricate forms and added colors and mingled effects to what had been mundane interiors just a decade previous. Nash introduced its "600" series, which made the company a pioneer in the mass production of unitized bodies. Then there was styling.

Much of it carried over from 1939. But there were some innovations. Lincoln's Continental was made available to the public for 1940. Only 50 convertibles and 350 coupes were made for buyers who could afford to spend about $3,000 for a fancy new set of wheels. The sporty Continental set an enhanced image for Lincoln. Packard also was innovative with its 1941 Clipper. Fade-away front fenders and a narrow but distinguished Packard grille, typical of the times, told onlookers that somebody was arriving in style. The car was wider than it was high and offered roomy comfort in the Packard luxury car tradition. The Clipper sold above the Packard "120" in the medium price class and below the "160" in the high price class. It was not a cheap car, and even the military placed an order for several hundred of the Clippers to be used as staff cars for high ranking officers.

The wheels of industry were in motion for defense production, and the experience would alter the industry. William S. Knudsen, who had served as the big wheel at Chevrolet and then General Motors, was in motion for the defense of his adopted country. The Dane was named Director General of the

A proud owner featured in a Packard ad campaign shows off his new 1942 Clipper club sedan. The revolutionary Clipper styling was introduced in April 1941 only as a four-door sedan. Sales skyrocketed. By 1942, the styling dominated the entire Packard line. Beginning with the Clipper body and continuing near the end of the 1954 model run, Packard bodies were built by Briggs Manufacturing.

Office of Production Management for the United States. He was to coordinate all defense production in the public sector. The auto industry, having one of its own in such a key post, responded favorably.

In April 1941, Alfred P. Sloan, Jr., chairman of General Motors, told Knudsen that GM's tool shops were offering their services for defense. "We propose to eliminate the yearly model change of passenger cars that we normally make, applicable to the year 1943. This means that the 1942 model, which goes into production this summer, will be continued through 1943. As you know, this is the time when we would ordinarily start our engineers, designers, and draftsmen working on plans for 1943. This change of policy at this time offers the possibility of accentuating the Defense Program on two vital counts that appear to me to be the most important limited factors. . . first, administrative and technical management, and second, tooling capacity.

"There would be released a very considerable amount of managerial technical talent that could be diverted to production and engineering problems involved in national defense. . . a reservoir of qualified and experienced technicians who could be used wherever defense needs might demand.

"We spend on an average model change from $35 million to $40 million. This involves tooling, almost entirely. Probably 90

When World War II ended, passenger car production resumed. Packard had stored much of its large production equipment outdoors and had to refit its Detroit plant. Hence, the Clipper styling was continued with only minor trim changes. Other car makers did likewise.

percent of this capacity could be diverted to defense purposes. In terms of production, there would be involved approximately 15 million man hours.”[2]

In 1940 Ford’s mass production ability was strained when it was asked to make the Rolls-Royce aircraft engine according to a schedule and an amount that Ford officials said were impossible. Packard officials were asked to examine the possibility, accepted the challenge, and offered design modifications for the engine to facilitate mass production. Dodge was busy building 20,000 trucks for the military. And the progenitor of the Jeep was tested in Fort Benning, Ga., eventually resulting in its mass production with a major contribution by Willys Motors, Inc., and Ford.

It wasn’t the first time that car makers were involved in defense production. In 1917 the entire American auto industry patriotically offered its services as the nation entered World War I. Aeroplanes were a new battle tool, and the Liberty engine built by various auto makers powered the crafts. There was talk that car production might be halted. Women entered the work force as men were drafted for military duty.

The most popular body style offered by Packard was for the 22nd Series and 23rd Series (which stretched from 1948 to 1950). The styling was a facelift of the Clipper and reflected the automotive tastes of buyers who went for an enveloping and streamlined look. Nash and Hudson also offered a similar approach to design.

Armaments, munitions, and military vehicles were mass produced while passenger car production continued alongside or nearby. White, Nash, and Packard made trucks. Fuel was conserved.[3]

The image of Cadillac grew thanks to its wartime participation in 1917 and 1918. Among 87 makes of American and foreign cars in use by the American Expeditionary Force in Europe, Cadillac became the preferred car for high ranking officers. Only 199 Standard Seven Passenger Cadillac touring cars were used by the military in the States while 2,095 went overseas. "The Army took the Cadillac touring car as it stood, without changing a line or altering a dimension," Cadillac reported. An emergency fuel tank was added to a running board and tire chains were carried. "Except for these minor changes and the olive drab finish, the Cadillac that was sent overseas was the same as the one which (was) seen daily on American streets and roads." Various military vehicles were made by Cadillac and other car makers for the war. That experience stayed with many

In 1948 Cadillac took a turn toward new styling that was fresh and awe inspiring to many luxury car owners. Even the rear end received notice with trend-setting finned taillights. For the 1949 Cadillac, shown here, minor updates were added to grille and trim, but the real news was the 331 cubic inch V-8 engine with 160 hp at 3800 RPM.

of the workers who, in more than a few cases, had progressed up the industrial ladder and could use that knowledge toward defense production for World War II. The auto industry was conditioned for the challenge.[4]

When Pearl Harbor was bombed on December 7, 1941, the industry was in for the long haul. Had it not been for the conversion from car lines to defense production, Detroit—and indirectly the entire nation—would not have been given the title, "Arsenal of Democracy" by Sir Winston Churchill. Every car maker jumped into the cause. For some, like Graham, it meant a reprieve from oblivion. For others, like Packard, it meant halting the momentum established by the new Clipper styling which for 1942 had progressed into the junior and senior lines. On February 9, 1942, all civilian passenger car production was stopped by the government. The national speed limit was dropped to 40 mph and later dipped to 35 to conserve fuel, recalling the "Motorless Sundays" that preserved fuel supplies during World War I. The Ford factories, which for a time took solace in pacifism, now were turning out huge bombers and other armaments. Gas rationing and tire restrictions followed.

In plants, work forces burgeoned to double or triple their number. Production ran at high rates, and workers almost always gave their extra effort. Some donated time and labor to produce an extra airplane or boat. Blood drives and bond drives were common among plants.

Cadillac revolutionized the high-price market with its rakish styling for 1948, which added upturned fins to the rear fenders. In 1949 this was to be followed by the innovative V-8 of modern configuration, which in updated versions would power Cadillacs for more than a decade.

Buick was about to redefine its place in the industry as the 1940s dawned. Six series and 26 body styles made up the 1941 line, epitomized here. Prices ranged from $735 for a Series 40-B business coupe to $2,465 for a limousine. Pressure from the GM ranks, notably Cadillac, encouraged Buick officials to set their sights on the medium price field rather than compete with stablemates.

Dealerships nearly closed up shop. It was not uncommon for a dealer to watch nearly all of his staff enter the service. One dealer, who had about 25 employees, saw his ranks diminish to himself as salesman, one or two clerks for the front office and sales department, and just a few mechanics who were beyond the draft due to age. Former personnel came out of retirement to see dealerships through the war. New cars were sold under government permission on a priority basis to doctors and for a few other necessary lines of work. The sale of used cars was regulated. Fewer were sold to dealers as values went sky high. Meeting the needs of car owners during World War II meant servicing their vehicles. Regular maintenance check-ups were encouraged by dealers, postcards were mailed to remind car owners to keep their cars running well "for the duration," and parts were sent to dealers under much scrutiny. When a factory stock of replacement parts was nearly depleted, the government had to grant permission for a limited run to replenish the stock.[5]

Stories circulated among American troops that the

Total sales of all GM products came to $2.4 billion for 1941; $3.8 billion for 1947; and $4.7 billion for 1948.

Soon ... they will be here!

Watch for first showings of exciting new 1946 Hudsons in your community

New car production is under way at Hudson.

It will be expanded as rapidly as conditions permit, until the full capacity of our great, modern plants is again devoted to the manufacture of automobiles.

There are many surprises in the first post-Victory Hudsons coming from our assembly lines. Fresh new colors. New appointments and fittings. New luxury and convenient features.

Underneath the style and smartness pictured here, you may count on all those solid qualities which have won so many new friends for Hudson during the difficult war years.

Reliability. Unfailing performance. Endurance. Low-cost operation.

There is an unprecedented demand for these 1946 Hudsons, among old friends and new. They will be distributed—fairly and evenly—across the nation, as production permits.

See these brilliant new cars at your earliest opportunity. You will be welcome at the showroom of the nearest Hudson distributor or dealer, to get full information about the motoring satisfaction that Hudson offers for the coming year.

HUDSON MOTOR CAR CO., DETROIT 14, MICHIGAN

HUDSON

The 1948 Tucker was torpedoed before it got to safe waters in sales. A mere handful were spread around the nation, causing heads to turn and often creating traffic problems when they appeared on streets. Only 51 of the Chicago-built cars were constructed, the company being the casualty of a government investigation that eventually exonerated Preston Tucker.

American was the best fighter in the war, and the automobile played a part in the boast. The American soldier was in robust health, took pride in his nation, was well armed, and had something the German or Japanese soldier did not have: a common knowledge of automotive mechanics. The popularity of the automobile in America encouraged backyard mechanics to develop, many since their youth. When machinery—including vehicles—broke down during the war, Yankee ingenuity and creativity often played a part in repairs. In Japan and Germany, automobiles were not nearly as common, and the population was, therefore, less versatile in the upkeep of motor vehicles.

With the capitulation of Italy and the fall of Germany, car makers knew the war was winding toward its conclusion. The U.S. government issued regulations allowing for the conversion to passenger car production to begin after V-E Day, May 8, 1945. But would Japan continue its battles throughout 1945 and into 1946? Would more defense production still be needed? When the atomic bomb hastened the surrender of Japan, some big wheels in the auto industry had to have been caught short. How soon could their production lines be putting out mass passenger car production similar to prewar days? Where would they secure raw materials?

Hudson whetted the appetite of car buyers by campaigning the return of passenger car production. Major ad themes in national magazines and numerous local newspapers encouraged buyers to wait patiently until freedom was safe.

Numerous new makes were announced during the heated sellers' market of the late 1940s. Among them were the sporty Playboy with retractable top, the Bobbi-Kar made with fiberglass and wood (and its later manifestation, the Keller), the three-wheeled Davis, and the Tucker. Preston Tucker's car was built with safety in mind, from pop-out windshield in the event of collision, to the rear-mounted Franklin-inspired engine, and to the directional center headlight. The car was unique. But on Sunday, June 6, 1948, after months of hectic preparation for production, the Tucker was torpedoed by Drew Pearson in his popular radio commentary. He claimed the car would never be produced beyond the "dream car" stage and that the company would be "blown higher than a kite." The public had become wary of false promises made by some of the new car makers.

In a letter to Attorney General Tom C. Clark issued the same day, Mr. Tucker said, "If Drew Pearson has presumed to speak for the Department of Justice without authority, with or without intent to cause us serious injury, we believe your department should take immediate cognizance of such action. . . the Tucker is not a 'dream car,' and we will have three cars in Washington Tuesday (June 8) which we assure you are neither myths or phantoms, and which we will be pleased to have both your department and Pearson examine at close range.

"For Pearson's personal action in this matter we are preparing a suit for damages suffered by our corporation and our stockholders and dealers. Our considered opinion is that approximately 50,000 American stockholders in the Tucker Corporation may lose from $5-10 million after the market opens Monday, and that in addition investments will be imperiled totalling millions of dollars to Tucker dealers in franchises and facilities." In a letter to stockholders, also dated June 6, Tucker added: "The Tucker Corporation is sick and tired of defending itself against repeated malicious and inspired attacks, and is determined no longer to be content with a mere defense." His words rang true, even after the Tucker car was stopped cold in its tracks. Eventually vindicated, Preston Tucker was still setting the record straight in the press as late as 1954. He died shortly thereafter.

Actual color photograph of New 1947 Studebaker Champion Regal De Luxe 4-door Sedan

Sweet and low... a melody in metal

...the completely new 1947 Studebaker

Here's the 1947 Studebaker Commander Regal De Luxe Coupe for five—Like all Studebakers, it's a standout in operating economy. Both Champion and Commander models are available in 4-door and 2-door sedans, 3-passenger and 5-passenger coupes. Alluring new 1947 Studebaker convertibles are coming shortly.

This is it—the new 1947 car that you've been hoping someone would build—a car even finer than you dreamed of.

That picture of it you see above is a color photograph of the real thing—the new 1947 Studebaker "in person."

Here's more than a car out ahead in point of time—it's unmistakably far ahead in distinctive postwar styling—completely new from every view—brand new bodies—advanced new chassis—a low, long, luxurious motor car that's a melody in metal.

Featured here is the big, roomy, new Studebaker Champion 6-passenger, 4-door sedan—and there's a full range of other thrilling body styles in Commander as well as Champion models.

These cars are ready months in advance, because Studebaker had the earnest co-operation of the finest group of employees in the motor car industry in producing them.

Go to the nearest Studebaker dealer's showroom and see these beauties right away. And remember, these 1947 Studebakers excel by far in riding comfort and handling ease as well as in exclusive smartness.

STUDEBAKER

First by far with a postwar car

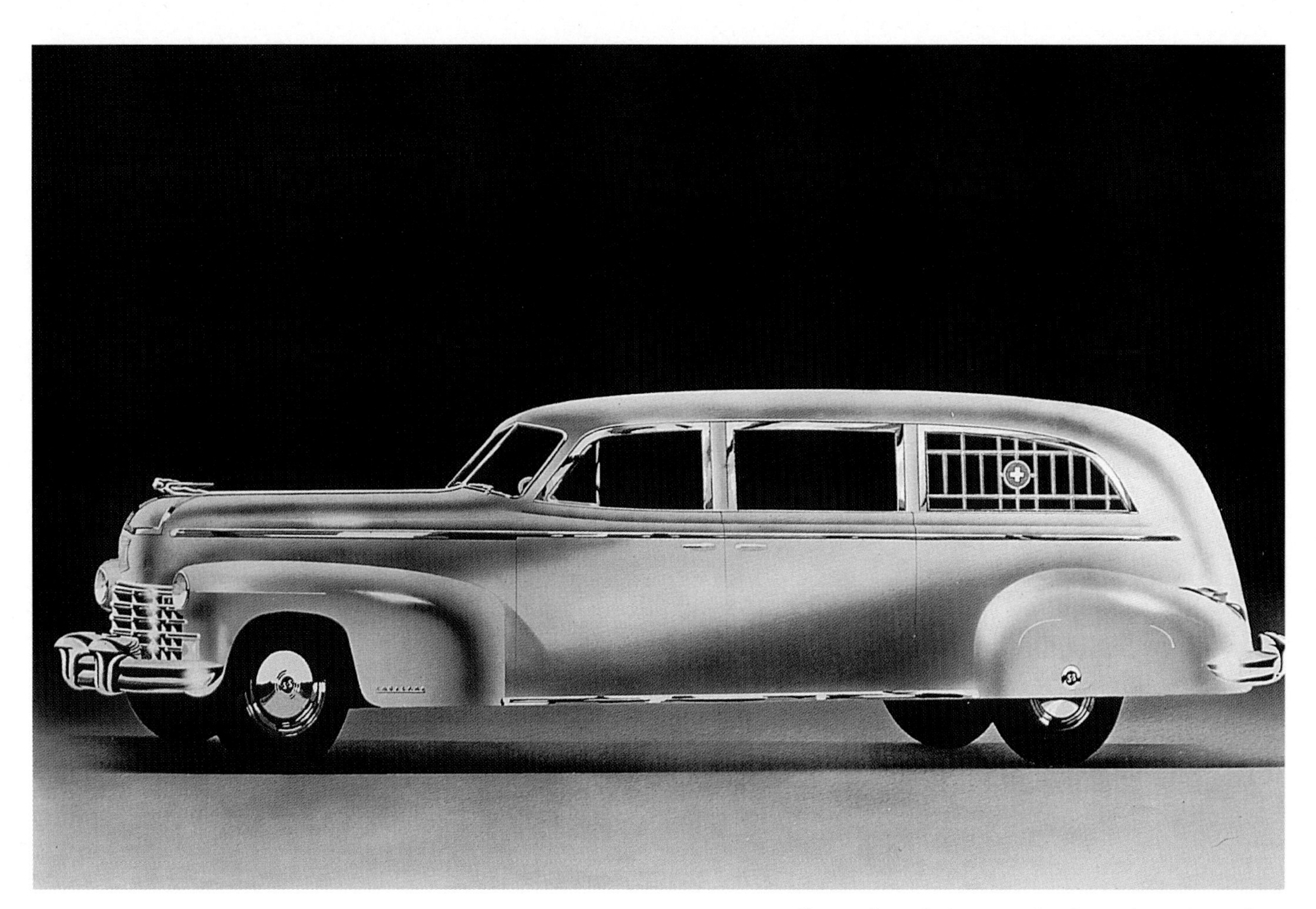

Following the end of wartime hostilities, the professional car trade jumped into production. Sayers & Scoville, Henney, Superior, Eureka, and others saw the promise for good profits. However, some makers, such as Miller, were caught in the steel shortage and had major retooling following their switch from defense production. It was a costly transition.

It was a challenge that Ford met first. On July 3 it began passenger car production. Just before, the Crosley Corporation announced it would produce a small four-cylinder car. Just after, the formation of the Kaiser-Frazer Corporation, which was to include the efforts of Graham-Paige Motor Corporation, was announced. When Japan surrendered on August 14, 1945, it was the last day for gas rationing. Restrictions on the production of trucks were lifted on August 20, and the 1946 models of new cars were in heated production. What slowed the process were work stoppages due to material shortages and union concerns.

Studebaker took the styling lead among mainline auto makers with its new postwar design for 1947. Sleek and offering high visibility for passengers and driver, the Studebaker design would last through various updates and facelifts for many years.

Willys-Overland received a new lease on its business life with the civilian version of the Jeep. In January 1948 the company promoted its new Station Sedan, "a glamorized version

Studebaker became a style leader after it offered its prewar warm-over for 1946. The 1947 Studebaker Champion was introduced in May of 1946.

Top, left: Henry J. Kaiser entered the car business as a West Coast entrepreneur who wanted to show the auto executives in Detroit that they did not have a monopoly on production. The 1947 Kaiser car, using the American buffalo or bison as its symbol, carried a large hood badge instead of a hood ornament. The ornament was quickly added, however, as a response to dealers and the public.

Top, right: Joining with Kaiser was Joseph Frazer, who headed what survived as Graham-Paige. The Frazer was the more expensive offering in the initial Kaiser-Frazer line, although Kaisers shared the same body through 1950. The Frazer badge was a coat of arms that remains the largest and one of the most intricate ever sported by a car.

Bottom: Frazer built on his reputation in the auto business as production neared. His connections with Chrysler had put him in solidly with many dealers nationwide, and this experience served well in setting up a dealer network for Kaiser-Frazer.

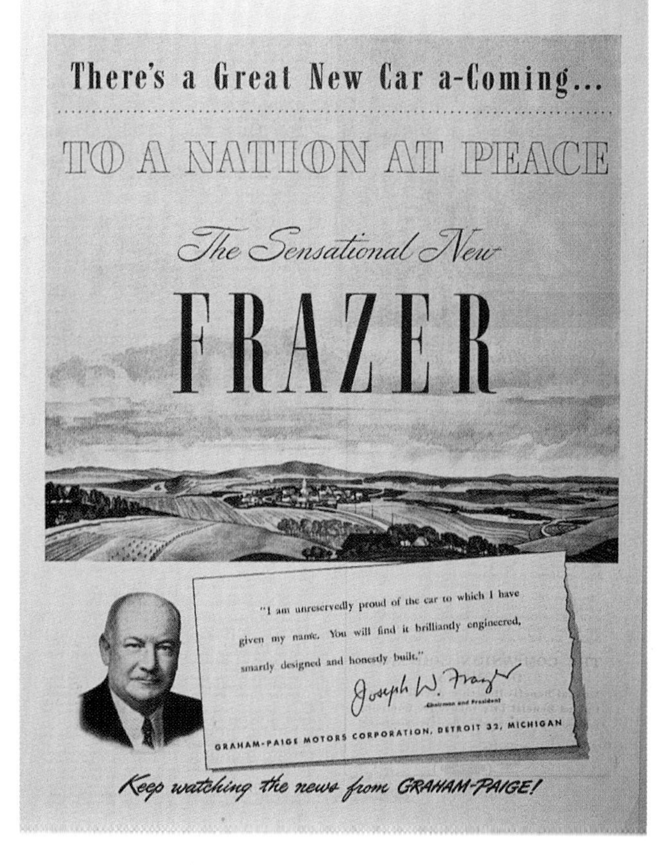

Colorful exteriors and plush interiors were hallmarks of the early Frazers. Slab-sided styling was to sweep the industry.

of the popular Jeep Station Wagon with its luxurious interior and its entirely new outside dress." Announced as the "glamour girl" of the Jeep line, it was the first six-cylinder car made by the company since 1932. It was also hailed as "the basis from which the company's postwar passenger car will be built." Jeep popularity had begun as legends were carried back home from the war. Soldiers who had seen the nearly miraculous performance of Jeeps over the roughest terrain amid heavy bombardment or winter's curse stood in awe of the workhorse. Their stories of the Jeep enhanced the reputation of the vehicle. Jeeps were not made exclusively by Willys-Overland during the war, but the design was owned by the company. When hostilities ceased, the door opened for civilian Jeep versions to be made. To facilitate deliveries, two distributors took 97 personnel to Toledo, Ohio, to tour the plant, see the new models, and drive away with 80 vehicles. That's how hungry dealers were for new vehicles![6]

Of the hundreds of manufacturers in the American auto industry, there were only 18 passenger car makers left in 1947.

Some of the most beautiful classic lines to appear on an American car came on the Cadillac for 1941. In convertible form it proved to be a sensation. The LaSalle concluded its production for 1940, its price range being absorbed by Cadillac. The intricate horizontal grille motif would predominate on Cadillacs for many years.

The 1941 60-Special was favored by fashion-conscious buyers. The model added to the make's drive toward success as the dominating force in the luxury car field.(Photo by M. Lawrence Hassel)

The last of its prewar updates came for Pontiac in 1948. The Streamliner and Torpedo series came with inline sixes and eights. The Torpedoes had a wheelbase of 119 inches; the Streamliners carried 122. Prices ranged from $1,500 from a closed car to just over $2,000 for a convertible, although the woody station wagon went as high as $2,490 in base price.

The sedanet or fastback styling, promoted by GM, was a popular feature of the 1940s. The tapered roof blended with the trucklid for a dashing appearance. Pontiac carried its Silver Streak trim on the hood and trunk as a styling statement. Fender guards, affixed to the bumper, were common extras pushed by salesmen and gave a higher margin of profit to dealers.

There were only 16 truck makers, too. So noted M. E. Coyle, executive vice president of General Motors, in a speech to automotive merchants in Atlantic City, N.J., October 3, 1947. "It has not been an easy road, this automobile producing business. . . . Could the automotive industry be organized and developed under conditions today? It could not, and neither can other important industries. . . . During the war years we produced 16 million less passenger cars and trucks for civilian use than would have been normal expectancy. In 1946 and 1947 combined, we are running at approximately the prewar rate on passenger cars, so two years in age has been added to the cars in operation and we still have all the pent-up demand before us. Truck production is about 50 percent above the prewar level, so the demand for trucks will be satisfied earlier than is the case in passenger cars. Our accomplishments, compared to what we anticipated, have been most disappointing."

Especially disappointing to Coyle was a coal strike that slowed down the recovery of production for all industries in the nation and affected home heating supplies. More strikes followed in other business realms and price hikes were certain.

"Labor rates that were 90 cents per hour in 1941 are now $1.50. . . the prices of automobiles have inflated less than farm products, and. . . are far below the level of most manufactured goods." But even though a new Pontiac in 1942 had sold for around $1,100 and its comparable version in 1947 sold for several hundred dollars more, the wages being earned by many Americans had risen to meet the demand. Peace was in the air, freedom reigned, and life was grand.

Business would be grand for the auto industry, too, at least for a while.

Notes

1. Oldsmobile data based on the report, *Confidential Data on Dealer Operation 1940 and 1939*, a two-part study by the Business Management Division, Oldsmobile Division, General Motors Sales Corporation, April 1941, courtesy of Jim Bennett.

2. From a General Motors news release dated April 19, 1941, which quotes Sloan's letter to Knudsen.

3. *Automobiles of America*, Automobile Manufacturers Association, 1970; pp. 64-67.

4. Facts and quotes taken from *Cadillac Participation in the World War*, a hardbound and oversized catalog issued by the Cadillac Motor Car Company in 1919.

5. Comments regarding dealership woes are taken from interviews the author had with Irv Albrecht, president of Albrecht-Burke Packard.

6. Comments about Willys-Overland are based on *W-O Sales News*, January 1948, a monthly magazine issued by the company.

7. Condensed from a Sun Oil Company accessory manual issued in late 1948.

MAKE A DATE WITH THE "88"
OLDSMOBILE

LOWEST-PRICED CAR WITH THE "ROCKET" ENGINE

*Above: Oldsmobile "88" Convertible Coupe. *Hydra-Matic Drive standard equipment on Series "98" and "88," optional at extra cost on "76." White sidewall tires optional at extra cost.*

Some day soon—it could even be tomorrow—*you'll* have your date with the "88"! You'll be standing in an Oldsmobile showroom, admiring those clean Futuramic lines—and your dealer will hand you the keys. Then it begins. You feel the "Rocket" Engine surge with Hydra-Matic* smoothness to highway speed—so eager—so quiet—hinting of so much more. You try the "88" in traffic. You discover its deft dexterity—the completely new *command* it gives you—with this compact new Body by Fisher. Then—before you know it—you're in the open! Miles spin under your wheels like minutes—you ride a great, gathering wave of "Rocket" Engine power—you find an exultant, air-borne freedom! That's *"The New Thrill"* you've waited for! So don't wait any longer. *Make a demonstration date with the Oldsmobile "88"!*

"The New Thrill"

FUTURAMIC

OLDSMOBILE

DIVISION OF GENERAL MOTORS

Chapter 7

After the Independents, What Next?

"Every new and proven element for passenger comfort, convenience, and safety has been engineered into the new models. We believe the Golden Anniversary Packards to be the best-designed cars in the company's 50 year record of fine-car building," noted William H. Graves, executive engineer for Packard. His comments were issued on April 28, 1949.[1]

Packard was the first of the car makers to reach its 50th anniversary and remain independent. Oldsmobile had existed longer, but it had been changed with the departure of R. E. Olds early in its history and then became part of General Motors. Packard was one of only a few makes that had not been absorbed into a conglomerate, and therefore carried the label "independent." In the same camp at the beginning of the 1950s were Studebaker, Nash, a tiring Hudson, a diminishing Willys-Overland, a failing Crosley, and the newcomer Kaiser-Frazer. Opposite these makers stood the mighty General Motors, the slipping Chrysler Corporation, and a revitalized Ford headed by Henry Ford II.

The 1949 Golden Anniversary Packard was touted by the company as having 77 "principal improvements and scores of 'hidden' technical changes never seen by the average owner." Most owners did not care, either, since the changes were so

Oldsmobile's Futuramic design, which was launched in 1948, rocketed the car into the 1950s. The overhead valve Rocket V-8 engine for 1949 carried a bore and stroke of ¾ by 3 7/16 inches and put out 135 hp at 3600 RPM. Coupled with a relatively light body the engine brought high performance to the medium-price field in the 1950s.

In the 1950s, unmodified passenger cars with large V-8 engines could run at top speeds close to 120 mph. Such was a reminder of the 127.88 mph run of a Stanley steam car at Daytona Beach, Fla., in 1906. Ordinary gasoline cars could now do as well as steam cars and maintain high speed running of 70 mph over vast distances without engine damage or major mechanical wear.

Jewels by Van Cleef & Arpels
IT'S A "CADILLAC AMONG CADILLACS"
There are many ways in which we could describe the new Golden Anniversary Cadillac. We could say, for instance, that it is the most beautiful Cadillac ever built—and as you can easily see, that would be right. Or, we could say that it is the most *luxurious* of all the Cadillacs—and if you could just open the door and look inside, you'd know instantly that this, *too*, is true. Or, again, we could say that it offers the finest *performance* in Cadillac's great history —and if you could only experience its tremendous power and its almost unbelievable responsiveness and handling ease, you would readily understand that this is likewise correct. But it seems to us that the best way to describe this wonderful Golden Anniversary creation is to say simply that it's a *Cadillac among Cadillacs*. We know, of course, that this is a tremendous compliment to pay a motor car. But we know, too, that it is a compliment most richly deserved. Why not come in today and see and drive this great new Standard of the World? We know you'll agree that it is a fitting climax to fifty years of ever-increasing quality and prestige.
THE GOLDEN ANNIVERSARY
Cadillac
STANDARD OF THE WORLD!
YOUR CADILLAC DEALER

Cadillac's 50th anniversary was commemorated in 1952. The GM division reached the buying public through a clever series of advertisements that hyped expensive jewelry to hallmark the make.

minute. What buyers saw was the innovative 1941 Clipper design made into a slab-sided style typical of the late 1940s. That update was issued for 1948, so when mid-1949 rolled around the design was anything but new. The company was selling on its reputation as the leading producer of fine cars in America. However, in 1950 Cadillac overtook Packard in sales for good.[2]

With its rear fins and trend setting overhead valve 331 cubic inch V-8 engine, with bore and stroke of 3 $^{13}/_{16}$ by 3 $^{5}/_{8}$ inches, Cadillac delivered a forceful 160 hp at 3800 rpm and aimed at meeting the needs of the buyer as never before. Packard, burdened with an aged leadership and a medium-price emphasis by the soon-to-retire President George Christopher (who had spearheaded Packard's entry into that price class with the "120"

IT GOES TO THE STADIUM . . . FOR EIGHT! This great new Plymouth Station Wagon sets new standards for beauty, utility and long life. Comfortably seats eight full-sized passengers. Both rear seats quickly and easily removed for maximum loading space. Handsome, easy-to-clean vinyl plastic seats and seat backs. Natural-finish bonded plywood body panels with long-life finish on all-wood surfaces. New body construction—new steel floor and top—make this the safest, most rugged Plymouth Station Wagon ever built—with Plymouth engineering throughout. Before you buy—compare!

PLYMOUTH

THE CAR THAT LIKES TO BE COMPARED!

WHAT SPORT . . . TO DRIVE IT! This beautiful new Plymouth Convertible Club Coupe features distinguished styling and all-weather comfort. Electric-hydraulic mechanism silently raises or lowers new, smartly styled top in about fifteen seconds. Roomy rear seat with plenty of leg room. New, more powerful 97-horsepower engine with seven-to-one compression ratio. Ignition key starting with electric automatic choke. The famous Plymouth Air Pillow Ride is now smoother than ever before! See your Plymouth dealer and see for yourself.

WHITE SIDEWALL TIRES, CHROME WHEEL COVERS, AND REAR FENDER SCUFF GUARDS OPTIONAL AT EXTRA COST.
The new, "double-size" rear window gives greatly increased vision. Zipper fastenings make it quickly removable.

Two ads show off the visual characteristics of Plymouth that held to a high-hat type of styling beginning in 1949 and well into the 1950s. Woody station wagons among all companies would become rare in the 1950s and eventually give way to all-steel construction pioneered by the Plymouth Suburban in 1950.

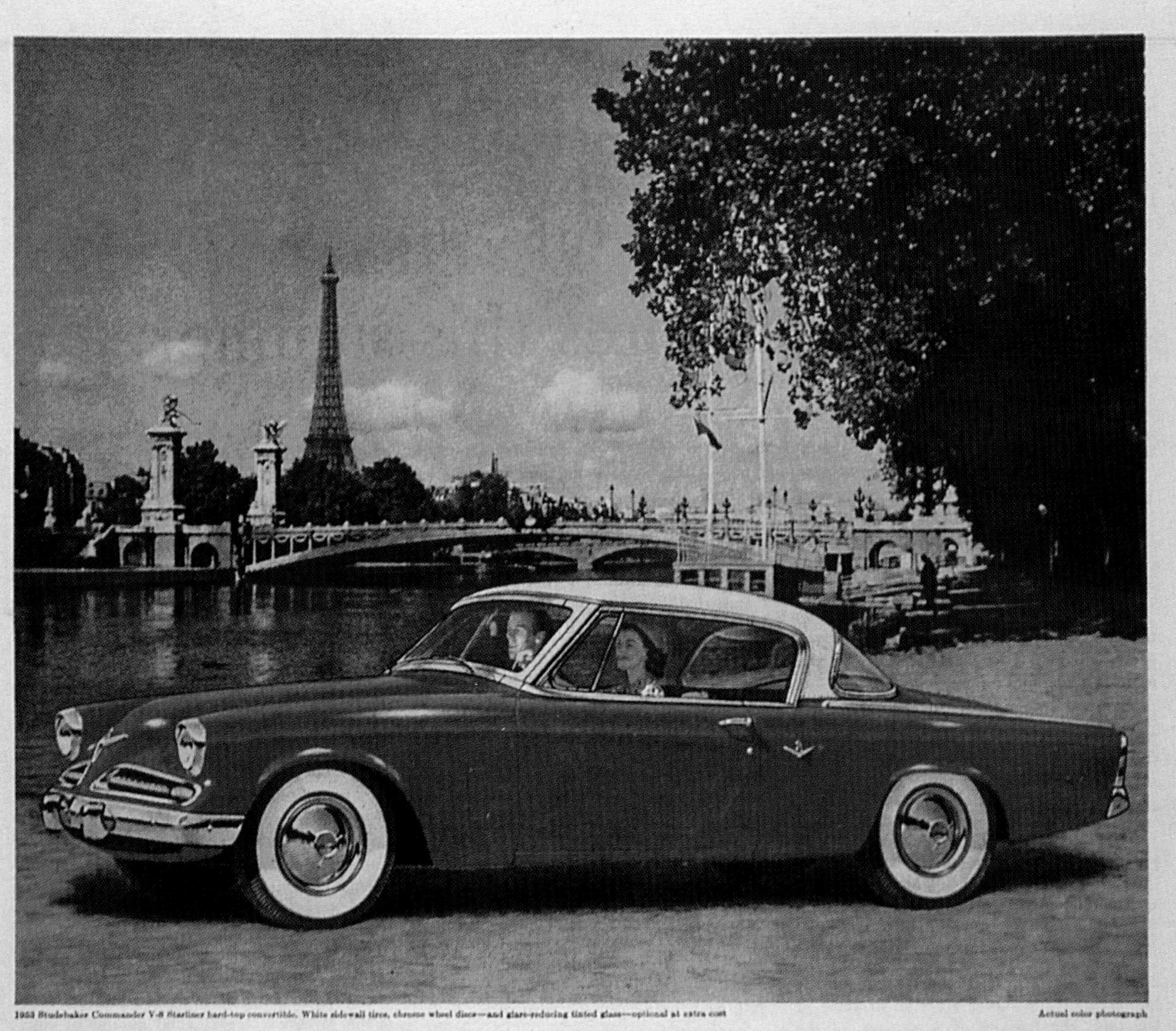

1953 Studebaker Commander V-8 Starliner hard-top convertible. White sidewall tires, chrome wheel discs—and glare-reducing tinted glass—optional at extra cost

Actual color photograph

the new American car with the European look!

It's the breath-taking new 1953 Studebaker!
Excitingly new in continental styling!
Impressively down to earth in price!

THIS dramatic new Studebaker comes to you straight out of the dream book.

It brings you the continental charm of Europe's most distinguished cars. But it's thoroughly American in deep-down comfort and in handling ease.

Long and racy and sparkling with drive appeal, every 1953 Studebaker gleams with an enormous expanse of glass for full vision. Every distinctive body style is completely and spectacularly new both inside and outside.

All this at a down-to-earth price—with Studebaker low operating cost!

Order your Studebaker now. Get a Champion in the lowest price field or a brilliant-performing Commander V-8.

Motoring's newest, finest Power Steering is available in Studebaker Commanders at moderate extra cost.

New 1953 Studebaker

It's a startler! It's a Starliner—the new 1953 Studebaker hard-top! Truly a new flight into the future! Less than five feet high!

Studebaker took on a European look and pushed it in 1953. Early in its history, the auto industry in America had allowed European styling to influence its designs, and the trend was picked up again in the 1950s.

In 1954 Studebaker and Packard had merged to survive. The 1956 Studebakers took on Packard-like echoes in certain trim touches to the grille, headlights, rear bumper, and taillights.

> The story has been told of a man who entered the Studebaker factory in South Bend once a week with a wheelbarrow. He would enter with it empty and leave with it full of parts. One week it might have been starters; the next week, carburetors. In time, the guards welcomed him cordially and expected his visit. This went on for some time until an official asked who this person was and what he was doing. It turned out that what he was doing had no connection to the factory. He was helping himself to parts. It also was not uncommon for factory workers to lift a part now and then off the line and take it home for family or friends to use on their Studebaker. Such occurrences became the target of control when Packard and Studebaker merged.[5]

and Six), never recovered. Even under lively management by President James Nance in the early 1950s, Packard only hoped to regain a modest portion of the high-class clientele.

Studebaker fared worse. For 1950, model year production was 320,884, which was a very high mark for an independent. However, 1952 production came to 167,662 and showed signs of dropping even more. The break-even point for expenses was unattainable. Even with its snappy European styling for 1953, Studebaker found itself deeper in the loss column as the decade progressed, unable to break from its high labor costs and production difficulties. Packard opted to buy Studebaker. What resulted in 1954 was a merger with Studebaker officials gaining sway. Although some innovative cars were made by both marques in Studebaker-Packard (with Clipper gaining its own recognition as a marque for 1956), the $38 million loss of Studebaker in 1954 and Packard's reorganization and over expansion in new plants resulted in the corporation nearly going

The 1956 Packard Patrician marked the end of large luxury car production for the marque. Only 3,775 Patricians were made that year, and its luxury companions consisted of the "400" hardtop and two Caribbeans (a convertible and a hardtop).

under in 1956 as the sales market hardened. What survived under a management contract with Curtiss-Wright of aviation fame had defense contracts and other assets bled from the corporation, effectively killed Packard, and allowed Studebaker to limp along with an occasional success—such as the sales-worthy Lark, the memorable Golden Hawk, and the classy Gran Turismo Hawk. Studebaker reached its conclusion as an auto maker in March 1966, by then having all its production in Canada.[3]

Kaiser-Frazer (K-F) absorbed Willys-Overland in April 1953. Henry J. Kaiser's dream of making a lasting mark on the automobile market had turned into a nightmare. The ship-building magnate and aluminum baron had even brought out the Henry J as a small car in hopes of retracing Henry Ford's steps of

Advertising had come of age in the 1950s and became a social influence like never before in the 1960s. Early in the century cars were advertised under several themes: the reputation or longevity of the manufacturer, uses and types of drivers, and basic features plus price. In the 1950s, the theme shift accentuated (1) the long, low, powerful aspects of American cars and how each year's cars were new and improved; and (2) performance, which ushered in the age of muscle cars. Ads on radio, television, billboards, and in print promoted a fantasy or image the buyer wished to realize through ownership. Liberal use of color and dramatic visuals were common and are summed up in a 1963 Ford ad, "These Super Torque FORD engines climb hills like a homesick Swiss yodeler; one is available with 425 hp (a few more than the average private plane)," and a 1964 Pontiac ad: "I wouldn't stand in the middle of the page if I were you. . . . It's a Pontiac GTO!"[6]

providing a car for the masses. But sales had worsened since the sellers' market had shifted to a buyers' market around 1950. Plus, Ford and Chevrolet were battling for first place in sales, a struggle that put the independent makers at risk of survival as their market shares plummeted. Model year production for K-F reached its height at 231,608 cars for 1951. For 1954 it was a paltry 10,097 and in 1955 it was a whimper at 1,291 Kaisers. Willys new car registrations had reached a postwar high point of 42,433 for 1953, only to drop to 6,267 for the last year of the marque. Defense contracts and the Jeep were the two promising aspects under the Willys banner.

Nash took over Hudson in 1954 to form American Motors. For 1948 Hudson had locked itself into its "step-down" design from the slab-sided school of styling and found it did not have

Above: Remaining similar in many respects from 1956 and into the early 1960s was the Studebaker Hawk. The Grand Tourismo would spring from this heritage and make for some classy lines as Studebaker limped to its end in 1966.

Opposite, above: The Hudson Stepdown design was innovative for the late 1940s, but grew unfashionable and difficult to update in subsequent years. For 1953 and 1954 Jet series was a smaller version of a popular package.

Opposite, below: Willys-Overland reached good sales achievements with its civilian Jeep and also dabbled with the Aero line from 1952 through 1955. Pictured is a 1948 Jeepster.

Hudson officials reflected the times in the Hudson Newsletter, November 1954, sent to Hudson owners: "Cupid's a back-seat driver—he must be, because a majority of 1,181 engaged or married men recently told an interviewer they proposed in an automobile. . . next to a car, the most popular proposal place is the front parlor." Also, "When you see an uplifted thumb at the side of the road, remember that two out of every five hitch-hikers are identified in the FBI's files."

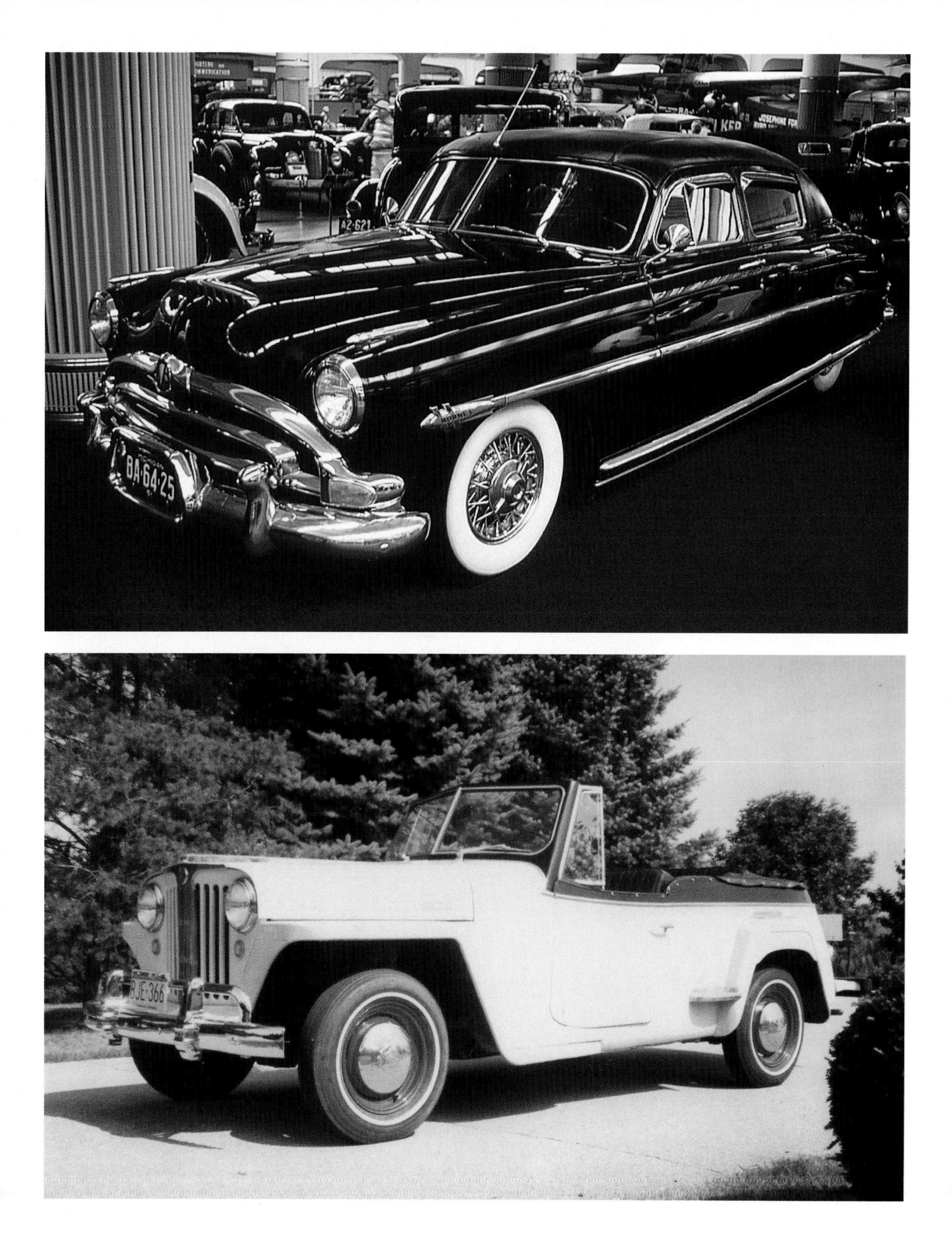

A2-621
BA·64·25
BJE·366

The New Car Season Starts Today!

Announcing The Brand-New Low-Price **Nash Ambassador Special V-8**
Engineered and Built By Nash With 3 Great New Travel Ideas...
1. *New Travel Roominess* 2. *New Travel Performance* 3. *New Travel Ease In Handling*

PRODUCT OF AMERICAN MOTORS

YOU HAVEN'T seen its like before—and you won't 'til the others catch up!

- **First big car to combine compact handling ease with spacious room. Biggest of all cars inside . . . regardless of price. Best big car in maneuverability . . . delightful to park.**
- **First in its Mobilgas Economy Run class in mileage—20.7 miles per gallon with new Flashaway Hydra-Matic Drive. First V-8 with high-torque pickup at all speeds.**
- **First in value with Single Unit Construction that lasts a "double lifetime"—assures higher resale.**
- **First in comfort with low-priced All-Season Air Conditioning . . . Airliner Reclining Seats . . . three-times smoother ride with Deep Coil Springs.**
- **First in safety with single unit construction. Frame is a steel, box-girder enclosure as big as the car; giving complete "wrap-around" protection.**

Enjoy this summer in the newest, coolest car that ever hit the road—the brand-new Ambassador Special Nash-built V-8. See it—the pattern of cars to come—at your Nash dealer's today.

SEE THE NEW
Ambassador Special
AT YOUR
Nash
DEALER NOW!
AMERICAN MOTORS MEANS MORE FOR AMERICANS
See Disneyland—great TV for all the family over ABC network.

The 1956 Nash Ambassador sold several hundred dollars less than comparable Hudson models, although the two makes shared the basic Nash body. In 1954 both marques formed American Motors Corporation.

When the Mercury Comet debuted for 1960, it was the marque's attempt to garner profits in the small car class. Sales achievements were very good the first year with more than 115,000 produced. The Comet continued to bring profits throughout the 1960s, although sales weakened. Pictured is a 1964 Caliente.

the finances to make a major new design in the 1950s. It needed a business partner. Nash, headed by George Mason and receiving financial support since 1936 from the merger with appliance innovator Kelvinator (from whence Mason came), saw the future in a full line of cars in every price class. Hudson dealers offered an attractive network for distribution. Mason's sudden death in 1954 and George Romney's rise to the presidency resulted in a redirection for AMC. Small cars and medium and lower-price offerings set the course for the corporation well into the future.

In the 1950s, Ford officials noticed a weakness in their company price structure: Too large a percentage of business was in the low price range. Officials wanted to offer a new model that was the best designed and engineered car of the 1950s and would span a major range of prices, thus filling the gaps. Called the E Car in pre-launch publicity, the car was years in the planning stage. The initial plan was approved by Ford's board of directors on April 15, 1955. Ford automobiles claimed 43.1 percent of the low-price field and Mercury and Lincoln had 13.6 percent of the upper-medium and lower high-price fields. General Motors was selling three brands in the price ranges Ford did not cover.[4]

The Edsel was to be Ford's answer. It offered electronic push-button transmission (similar to the Packard system of 1956), luxury appointments and gadgets galore, and color combinations

The 1955 DeSoto, with rakish looks and hot-performing Hemi Firedome V-8, would not be enough to save the marque from oblivion. The last DeSoto was unveiled for 1961 and quickly—and quietly—faded away as Chrysler Corporation revamped its market coverage.

The first Edsel hit the market for 1958 amid a massive fanfare of advertising by Ford. However, the car, even for all its strong points, seemed to miss its intended sales target and was discontinued with the 1960 model. Shown here is a 1958 Citation Edsel.

inside and out that seemed beyond the range of the rainbow. The Edsel was launched for 1958, the same year Ford marked the 50th anniversary of the first Model T.

Preliminary to the Edsel, in 1956, Ford launched the Continental Mark II hardtop coupe, a marvelously extravagant

With wood panels on the rear quarters, this Studebaker design buck had clay applied by the design department as planning for new models began. Other car makers in the 1960s did likewise in their styling studios.

Chrysler for 1964 offered razor-like lines, big car luxury, good handling with front torsion bars, and economy in the Newport line, seen here.

and costly car to produce. It was to take the stratospheric price range of $10,000 and appeared in some respects to be a large styling version of the Ford Thunderbird of the same year. Extreme in precision manufacturing and workmanship, it was meant to meet the needs of the wealthy. What it did was strain corporate finances but give the name Lincoln a renewed prestige as it took attention from the Cadillac Eldorado.

Remaining as the dominating force in the American automobile industry by the late 1960s were the Big Three: GM, Ford, and a weak but hopeful Chrysler. AMC was to broaden its base by absorbing Kaiser Jeep Corporation on February 5, 1970. The Jeep would bring financial gain to AMC for many years and

Although Henry Ford's experts were experimenting with the use of soybean and plastics for car bodies in 1941, it wasn't until the 1950s and 1960s that plastic-bodied cars gained in popularity. The efforts of Chevrolet's Corvette beginning in 1953, the Kaiser-Darrin for 1954, and Studebaker's Avanti introduced for 1963 brought fiberglass construction to the general public. The Corvette was based on the 1952 EX-122 dream car in the GM Motorama show that thrilled thousands of spectators as it toured the country. The first Corvette was built on June 30, 1953, in Flint, Mich. There would be 315 made before construction was moved to St. Louis, Mo. While officials predicted there could be more than 1,000 built per month, production for 1954 reached 3,640. At $3,498 for 1953 and $3,523 for 1954 the price was substantial for a six-cylinder car. For 1955, only 700 were made and the new V-8 engine was an option. Price: $2,934 with $135 more for the V-8 package.

Kaiser-Darrin was a one-year car, innovative with sliding doors that nestled inside the front fenders. The six-cylinder sports car was announced on September 26, 1952, and prototypes were unveiled on February 22, 1953. Only 435 were made and the selling price was $3,655. Actual sales to the public were launched January 6, 1954. The Avanti, available in two-door hardtop form, sold for $4,445 in 1963. Its 289 cubic inch V-8 could be supercharged for added performance. Highly successful for a car of its type in relation to its fiberglass predecessors, there were 3,834 made the first year. But for 1964, production fell to 809. That same year 8,304 Corvette two-door fastback coupes and 14,925 two-door convertibles were sold. The fiberglass car had come of age.

For 1956, Chevrolet continued its magic. Topping production for the model year was the "Two-Ten" four-door sedan with 283,125 units; the Bel Air four-door sedan with 269,798; and the "Two-Ten" two-door sedan, shown here, with 205,545.

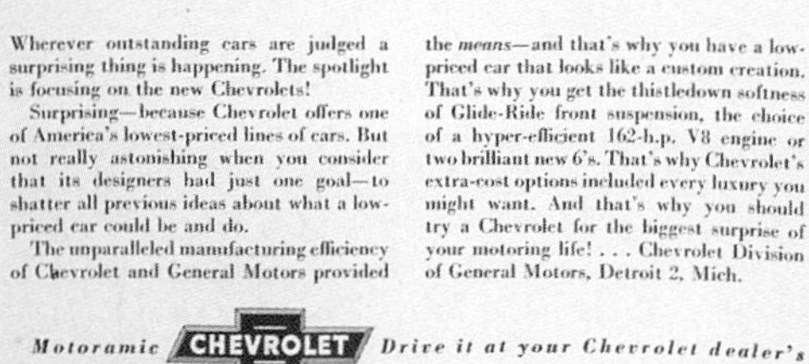

Chevrolet Bel Air Convertible with Body by Fisher.
Blue-ribbon beauty
that's stealing the thunder from the high-priced cars!
Wherever outstanding cars are judged a surprising thing is happening. The spotlight is focusing on the new Chevrolets!
Surprising—because Chevrolet offers one of America's lowest-priced lines of cars. But not really astonishing when you consider that its designers had just one goal—to shatter all previous ideas about what a low-priced car could be and do.
The unparalleled manufacturing efficiency of Chevrolet and General Motors provided the *means*—and that's why you have a low-priced car that looks like a custom creation. That's why you get the thistledown softness of Glide-Ride front suspension, the choice of a hyper-efficient 162-h.p. V8 engine or two brilliant new 6's. That's why Chevrolet's extra-cost options included every luxury you might want. And that's why you should try a Chevrolet for the biggest surprise of your motoring life! . . . Chevrolet Division of General Motors, Detroit 2, Mich.
Motoramic CHEVROLET Drive it at your Chevrolet dealer's

Setting a new direction in neo-classic design and with a modern V-8 engine was the 1955 Chevrolet.

allow the company to transfer the four-wheel-drive principle to passenger cars.

What triggered the industry as an element for success was a refinement of the source of power. Internal combustion gasoline engines gained industry favor in V-8 form in the 1950s and dominated the 1960s. Chrysler's Hemi engine for 1951 had taken that company into the horsepower race opposite the performance V-8s of Oldsmobile and Cadillac. The last American straight eight engines in mass production were under the hoods of Pontiac (which had offered a V-8 for several months in 1932) and Packard in 1954, reaching epic dimension with the latter at 359 cubic inches and 212 hp at 4000 rpm. Engine sizes and ratings were increased with fervor throughout the 1960s. The age of muscle cars had come.

So had the age of small cars. The diminutive Crosley did not survive as a make to enjoy the pleasure of watching a trend flourish. The small Henry J failed before America caught up to the fashion. AMC brought out its downsized Rambler for 1958 and made a hit. The even smaller Metropolitan made its mark on the industry. The result was a mad dash by the Big Three into the

Practically the same for 1953 and 1954—right down to the six-cylinder engine—was Chevrolet's Corvette, GM's major entry in the fiberglass-bodied field. From 300 Corvettes in 1953 to 3,650 for 1954, the model broke 6,000 in 1957, 10,000 in 1961, and 27,000 in 1966. For 1969, 22,154 sport coupes and 16,608 convertible coupes were made.

Mustang hit the market with a gallop in 1964 and never seemed to tire in sales. This 1965 Mustang epitomized the desire for carefree and sporty motoring, which Americans unleashed in numerous Ford showrooms.

small car field. Among the success stories was the Chevrolet Corvair, an air-cooled foray into the new field. About 1.8 million Corvair cars, wagons, vans, and trucks were made. (The only other time Chevrolet had offered an air-cooled car was with the Series C for 1923, which was a mechanical millstone.) By 1960 there were 10 American makes in what was then called the compact car category.

The 1950s and 1960s saw refinements in transmissions, electronic options, interiors, brakes, and—especially in the 1960s—to exterior styling with less brightwork, lower silhouettes, and sleeker bodies. Unusual features—such as retractable hardtops—were tried out by Ford.

Milestones were reached and notable beginnings were made. The fiberglass Corvette brought sports-car dash to Chevrolet dealerships beginning in 1953. What was initially known as "convertible hardtop" styling came to dominate the 1960s in two-door and four-door forms. Front-wheel drive re-entered the American scene. Chevrolet produced its 44 millionth vehicle in 1961. That same year DeSoto was discontinued, a casualty to the downward pricing of Chrysler and the upward pricing of Plymouth. General Motors made its 75 millionth vehicle in

In the late 1960s the Plymouth Barracuda set a high standard for speed and agility as the muscle car trend reached new heights.

1962. That same year Ford Motor Company was the first maker to reach the 30 million mark in V-8 production, and Shelby American, Inc., in Los Angeles, launched its Cobra, powered by the famous Ford V-8 engine. After 31 years Marmon-Herrington Company quit the automotive business in 1963. In April 1964 the Ford Mustang arrived and would change American motoring by putting a sporty car within the price reach of most buyers. About a month later the fastback-styled Plymouth Barracuda bowed as a direct answer to Mustang. In 1963 the fiberglass bodied Studebaker Avanti, a luxury sports car, took to the streets. It would outlive its first parent corporation and continue through the decade as the Avanti II.

The age of experimental cars had come in the 1950s and would continue for many years as car makers displayed various crowd-pleasing and futuristic concept cars at auto shows. Chrysler experimented with turbine-powered cars. General Motors produced more than 4 million vehicles in the 1964 model year, the first time such a milestone had been reached by any company. In 1965 the Rambler Marlin was AMC's answer to the Mustang and Barracuda and sported front disc brakes as standard. To gain favorable public opinion for its plans, General Motors showed glimpses into the future with its "Parade of Progress," which was held almost every year from 1936 to 1961. The mobile show reflected the spirit of innovation that had sparked the hearts of auto pioneers.

In 1966 the Excalibur, a replica of the 1927-30 Mercedes-Benz SSK Sports Car, was being claimed a success. In 1966 a

What would the Avanti by Studebaker have looked like by the late 1960s and in two-door and four-door form? Here is a company mock-up seen from the front, a relic from Studebaker days.

resurrected and scaled down Cord based on the 1937 Sportsman model was produced in Oklahoma City (about 100 would be produced) and the Stutz Motor Car Company of America announced in 1969 that a new Stutz Bearcat was to be manufactured. These cars were representative of a growing trend for assembled cars made by new businesses and using designs from the past.

Checker Motors Corporation was the only American auto maker to offer diesel engines on its taxicabs and passenger cars in 1968. That year the Monte Carlo, a prestigious Chevrolet, carried that make's longest hood, which measured six feet, and the Oldsmobile 4-4-2 gained series status. By the end of the decade, AMC's Javelin, Rebel, and AMX reflected the company's seriousness in the sporty field. A new car registration record was set for the American auto industry in 1968: 9,403,862.

Pioneers who passed away in the 1950s and 1960s included Edgar Apperson (1959), Walter Austin (1965), Frank Briscoe (1954), Abner Doble (1961), George P. Dorris (1968), Frank Duryea (1967), Andrew L. Dyke (1959), Herbert H. Franklin (1956), Charles B. King (1957), Charles F. Kettering (1958), Ransom E. Olds (1950), and Alfred P. Sloan, Jr. (1966).

The industry they had fostered was now taking a turn toward speed and performance like never before. It was also about to face perhaps the greatest challenge in its first century of existence. And that challenge was to come from overseas.

Notes

1. Taken from the Packard Golden Anniversary press kit, which included nine photos with captions, seven press releases, and three ad mats for newspapers. The writers of the press material seem hard pressed in taking minor features and elevating them to milestone status, except for the truly revolutionary Ultramatic transmission. The press kit noted that "Packard typifies once again the competitive, free enterprise which has made this country great!" Such press kits were issued once a year on a limited basis by car makers in the 1950s.

2. Packard's bathtub design has often been called "pregnant elephant" among collectors. This term was not widespread when Packard was in business. Dealers said it was not used in their circles and original owners have commented likewise. The term evidently was a derisive internal phrase used by very few in factory management. Its wide usage today is not historically accurate. Torsion-Level ride (full torsion-bar suspension), a Packard-engineered V-8, and the Ultramatic were three major innovations Packard fielded in its move to reclaim a good portion of the luxury market.

3. An excellent study of Studebaker-Packard is covered in *The Fall of the Packard Motor Car Company*, James A. Ward, Stanford University Press, Stanford, Calif., 1995.

4. *Ford: Decline and Rebirth 1933-1962*, Allen Nevins and Frank Ernest Hill, Charles Scribner's Sons, New York, 1963; pp.384-387.

5. Comments shared with the author in the 1970s via a Studebaker historian who had lived in South Bend, Ind., and had heard horror stories like these from former company employees.

6. Comments based on observations made in *Advertising in America, the First 200 Years*, Charles Goodrum and Helen Dalrymple, Harry N. Abrams, Inc., Publishers, New York, 1990; pp. 232-241.

Chrysler said its cars for 1954 were sleek, but the 1955 versions would be even more stylish. Here is the last of the body design that was based on initial tooling by Briggs Manufacturing, a company that supplied numerous bodies to car makers for many years until it was bought by Chrysler.

Auto shows became big business by the mid-1980s. Flashy displays, neon lights, computer-generated visuals, and tens of thousands of dollars for display settings became standard fare.

Chapter 8

Crossroads!

What Japan and Germany failed to do to America in World War II was nearly accomplished 35 years later. America was invaded and under siege. It wasn't a military encounter but an economic and industrial attack that changed the industry.

Thousands of small cars of all price classes made up the invasion force. It was a counter move against a "bigger is better"

Cycle cars represented the first serious small-car craze in America. They often were little more than two motorcycles with a common platform and allowing space for the driver and one passenger in tandem seating. Some like this 1914 air-cooled Scripps-Booth Rocket ($385), even steered from the back seat!

mentality, which had profoundly directed America's acceptance of the automobile since its inception.

The Volkswagen was among the first wave in the attack. Adolph Hitler dreamed of a German-made car for the people, which would sustain nationalistic pride. He had been impressed by the no-nonsense reliability of the Czech Tatra that he had used during his rise to political power. Ferdinand Porsche was one of several notables involved in the design of the Volkswagen (known as the KdF-Wagen) in the 1930s. Influencing the outcome was Hitler himself, suggesting the car's design in his own sketches and demanding that it be air cooled and of "robust" construction. In the mid 1930s it was Hitler's edict that the car was to sell for less than $1,000 marks ($250 U.S.). In 1938 the VW had taken form. But war soon put some unavoidable road blocks on the VW's initial road to success.[1]

After World War II and the passing of Hitler, Germany was given the opportunity to advance itself through free enterprise under Allied guidance. Factories of various industries were rebuilt. For 1946 the VW facilities in Wolfsburg produced 10,020 Beetles, each at a selling price of 5,000 marks. The cars were sent to European nations and truly delivered reliable service. The Model T Ford had been rediscovered in principle,

By 1988, Jeep was under the Chrysler banner. At auto shows it seldom was found in the middle of the glitzy, high-tech displays. The Hummer, acclaimed as the Jeep of the late 20th century, was made popular in the short Gulf War with Iraq. The vehicle also made it to auto shows in the 1990s. However, the high price of the specialty vehicle and its massive size seemed to be hindrances to widespread acceptance compared to the Jeep following World War II.

only this time the Beetles carried air cooling similar to the Franklin. The first Beetle was shipped to America in January 1949. By 1951 more than 40 percent of VW production was being exported to 29 countries. However, the U.S. market mentality was still geared toward big cars. So it was believed that 800 VWs would saturate the market!

This modest saturation point for the VW reached a new level when the 150,000th was delivered to America in 1960. That year the Beetle was selling in 136 lands!

The American auto industry had to take note as it stood at a crossroads for the future. The result was the small car trend of the late 1950s and early 1960s. But this was not America's first flirtation with small cars.

Long before the Lark and Metropolitan, the more recent Rambler, the Crosley, and the American Austin and Bantam had come the cyclecar craze. In 1914—and lasting for only a few years—America was fascinated with low-riding, low-cost, two-passenger vehicles, hardly appearing to be much more than a glorified motorcycle often with a minuscule car body, offering tandem seating and using four bicycle-inspired wire wheels. More than 40 cyclecar makers were taking their production seriously in America, organizing into associations to promote the

Front-wheel drive became popular in the 1980s. The system was promoted as offering better handling and allowed for lower construction as the age-old differential was removed from the rear wheels and the traditional drivetrain was dropped.

The concept was not new. The Front-Drive automobile was in the planning stage in 1905, with a proposed introduction as a runabout and light touring vehicle for 1907: "There is one great advantage in the front-drive automobile and that is that it will not skid in turning a sharp corner at a rapid rate of speed."[7] Weight reduction was also noted. The car was to sell for $550. It is likely it was not produced past the prototype stage. The front-drive design employed chain drive to the front wheels. Most of America was skeptical of the unconventional concept, although many auto experts likened it to the front-drive of a horse pulling a buggy. J. Walter Christie experimented with front-wheel drive and pioneered its development. In 1914 front-wheel drive surfaced in the Rex cyclecar of Detroit, which used a friction transmission that gave power to the front left wheel.

In 1929 the L-29 Cord and the Ruxton were introduced, each with front-wheel drive. The Cord was priced from $3,095 to $3,295 in sedan and brougham versions, respectively. It was aggressively promoted by Errett Lobban Cord who had taken over Auburn and Duesenberg with the money and experience he had gained with Moon as its top salesman in Chicago. The Ruxton was a last-gasp attempt by the Moon Motor Car Co. and L. Kissel & Sons. The Ruxton sold for $3,195 in either roadster or sedan versions, and a phaeton and town car were advertised. Launched amid the uncertain economic climate of 1929 especially in light of the Crash on Wall Street, much of the buying public was determined not to chance good cash on the purchase of an unconventional front-wheel drive car. Decades later, the concept of front-wheel drive had come of age.

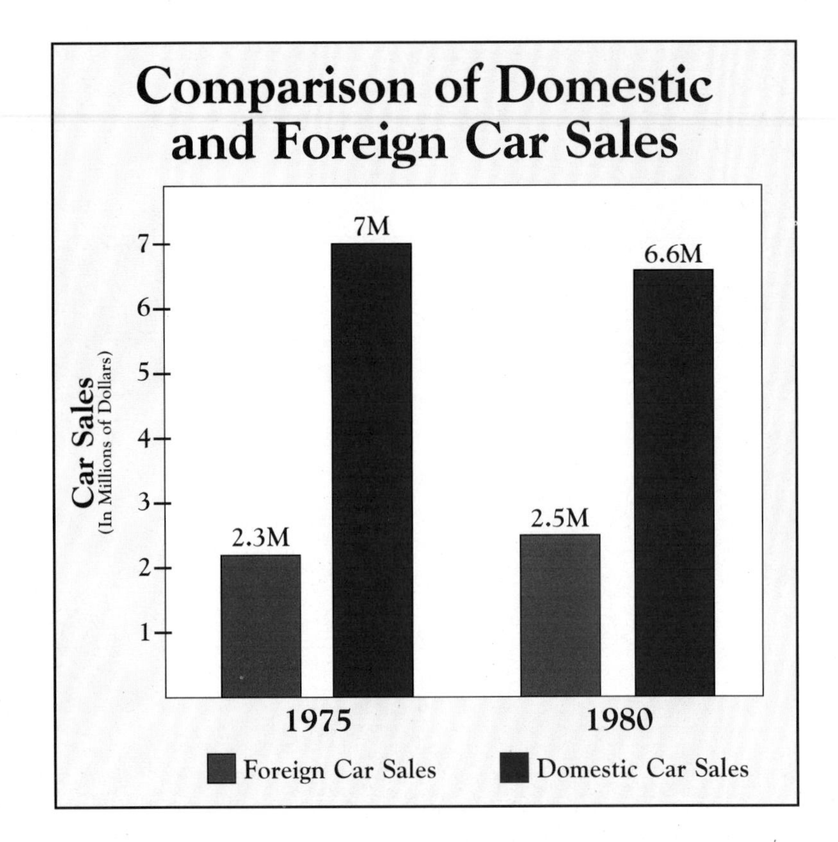

fad. Massive exports to Europe and Cuba were envisioned. In Australia, the American cyclecar was being hailed as "exactly what our people want." A network of 1,500 sales outlets were in place for Australia, New Zealand, Honolulu, and South Africa. But first the demand had to be met in America.[2]

It was, but much too quickly. The market soured and the craze subsided. One automotive expert in 1914 noted the seeds of failure that had been sown by cyclecar makers: "Complaint has been made that the cyclecar industry in this country has already seen too much of a boom, that it has been boosted too fast, that there had not been enough of care and try-out of cars, that the public had been, to some extent, fooled, that agents have been disappointed in the matter of deliveries—all of which is so to a limited extent."[3] Among the cyclecar makes that briefly flourished were the Imp of Auburn, Ind., the Comet of Indianapolis, Ind., the O-We-Go of Owego, N.Y., the Cyclette of Nashville, Tenn., the Duryea Cyclecar of Philadelphia, Pa., the Zip of Davenport, Iowa, and the Motokart of New York City, N.Y.

The VW was a much more sophisticated car than the cyclecar, and through use it had proved to be a rugged, reliable, low-cost form of transportation. It succeeded where other small cars had failed to make an impact on the industry. American car makers felt the VW was a fad and would not last. Other car makers, especially in Japan and France, took

Clenet was one of several specialty car builders that gained the attention of the press in the 1980s. Most of the cars sported modern running gear coupled with neo-classic styling.

notice. The sale of small foreign cars in America grew steadily in the 1960s and 1970s.

Small foreign cars that had been "trendy" had become a major selling force by 1980. Their upward move in the market accounted for 2.3 million in 1975 against domestic sales of seven million. For 1980 there would be 2.5 million imported cars and half a million imported trucks selling in America, against 6.6 million domestic cars and 2.4 million domestic trucks. This was the worst domestic sales level since 1961. The threat from overseas was not subsiding. It was no fad.[4]

Protectionism was rampant in America. Since car makers could not stem the sales tidal wave from offshore, the government was asked to protect domestic car makers through tariffs and trade controls. A comeback year was predicted for 1980, but those dreams faded when production in U.S. and Canadian plants slipped by 29 percent below the 1979 level and 36 percent under the record level of 14.7 million vehicles in 1978. Nearly three million less cars were made for 1980 than in 1978.

Such figures spelled doom. A half million fewer jobs were predicted for the American car industry for the early 1980s and

Even though the Chrysler Corp. suffered severe uphill battles to remain intact amid sluggish sales years and against overseas manufacturers, it put its best foot forward in public displays. Male and female models were paid and trained in telling the corporate story at auto shows.

an astounding number of car dealers were going out of business. In 1980 more than $4 billion was lost by General Motors, Ford Motor Co., Chrysler Corp., and American Motors!

The automotive invasion by Japan had become overwhelming by 1980. Japan accounted for 80 percent of imported cars. The advance in sales was like climbing a mountain, ledge by ledge. In 1969 Toyota recorded only 130,044

Is aerodynamic styling a good sales tool? Testing has revealed that with the reduction of wind drag against a vehicle comes an increase in gas mileage, better handling, and less noise for passengers. But some car experts claim that the emphasis on aerodynamics is overdone. Unless a car is driven great distances, major savings in fuel costs may not be realized based solely on aerodynamics. Also, high speed driving brings the most benefits in aerodynamics but many drivers seldom exceed 70 or 80 mph for prolonged distances. Some sales experts say it is better to have the factories produce cars which offer good styling than it is to make cookie-cutter cars which are hard to tell apart, all for the sake of aerodynamics.[8] The second century of the American automobile industry may very well determine the significance of aerodynamic styling.

sales in the United States. This jumped to 208,315 for 1970 and continued to climb, fostered by the national scare of a fuel shortage. Americans believed they now needed cars that were miserly on gas. Toyota passed the half-million mark in 1977 (576,728), the 600,000 point in 1979 (637,891), and for 1980 sales stood at 713,843. Toyota led the Japanese car pack with Datsun in second and Honda third. The tide had surged against

In the early 1960s Ford showed its Mustang idea car and tested the reaction.

the German makes in the recession of 1974. VW, Porsche, and Audi had accounted for 550,509 sales in America for 1973 but declined thereafter to only 145,716 for 1980.

What could the American auto makers do? Advance planning had been directed to large, stately, luxurious cars with monstrous horsepower. At the close of the 1960s, the buyers of small imported cars were being viewed less and less as anti-patriotic and not in the mainstream of American life. By 1980 owning a small foreign car was almost the norm. The American car industry had not acknowledged this trend and failed to meet the needs of many buyers. In so doing, the formula for success was being spoiled and the crown of sales leadership was being passed to a new king: Japan.

U.S. car makers counterattacked by bringing to their shores cars of foreign origin but under the badges of American makes: Ford carried the Fiesta, Capri, Cortina, Pantera, and Courier. Chrysler had its Colt, Arrow, and Cricket. AMC would side with Renault. GM would pander to the likes of the Buick Opel. Sales successes often were not as great as Detroit hoped and needed.

Another of the key elements for success had been changed.

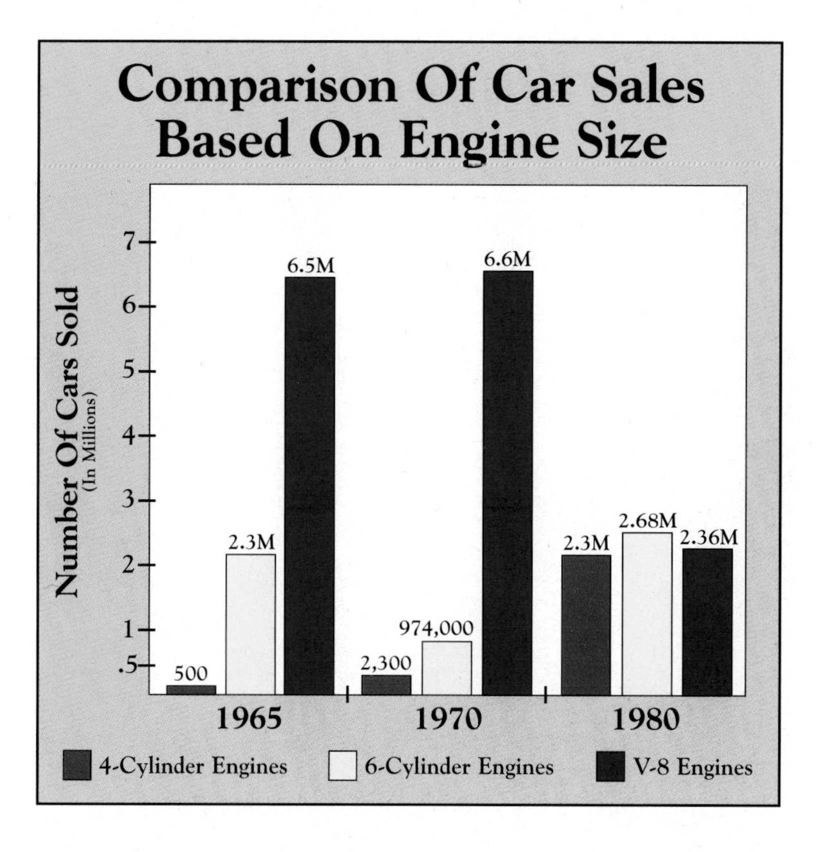

In motive power the four-cylinder engine was preferred almost equally to the V-8. In 1965 the four-cylinder car was almost dead. Only about 500 were made in America, compared to more than 2.3 million six-cylinder cars and nearly 6.5 million V-8s. For 1970, the figures were 2,300 (for the four), 974,000 (six), and 6,610,000 (V-8). Then the public changed its mind again and the four was back in demand. For 1980 the four-cylinder passed the 2.3 million point; the six was at 2.68 million; the V-8 held second place with nearly 2.36 million units.[5]

Cars with large engines peaked and declined. From the high point in 1970 of nearly 18 percent of new domestic cars with engines having a displacement of 401 cubic inches or more, the figure dropped to 4.9 percent for 1979. There were none registered for 1980. By 1980, more than 45 percent of all new U.S. cars carried displacements of 200 or less cubic inches; 20 percent carried displacements of 201 to 250; and just under 20 percent were between 301 and 350. Only a paltry 3.9 percent were 351 to 400 cubic inches, down from the high mark of 25.7 percent for 1972 and 1973.

There were changes in the luxury car field. For 1988, sales by foreign makes had cut into the market: Acura accounted for almost 109,500 sales; Mercedes-Benz was around 90,000; BMW claimed about 88,000; Porsche had around 23,600; and Jaguar stood with nearly 23,000. By the 1990s, Mercedes-Benz was giving Americans a new taste in luxury: smaller was better.

Since the 1980s, America has witnessed the rise of the mega-dealer. As the industry weakened, changed, and rebounded, car dealerships were involved in the struggle. Many succumbed. Others were absorbed by dealers who appeared to form sales empires crossing over various makes and encompassing several choice locations. Volume sales became necessary for survival, even in small towns. With the nearly unbounded outreach of radio and television advertising, dealers have sought sales well beyond what had been traditional geographic sales borders.

The attrition rate for domestic car dealers has taken a dreadful toll. In 1947 there were 45,580 dealers. That figure rose to 49,173 in 1949. From that point there was almost a continuous decline. In 1955 there were 40,374 dealers; in 1960 33,658; in 1970 27,071; and in 1980 23,379. In 1990 there was a good sign: 24,198 dealers were in business. But the slip resumed afterward, dropping below the 20,000 point to 19,065 in 1991. In the 1979 to 1981 recession there were about 1,800 dealerships which folded. During a similar recession, from 1989 to the end of 1991, nearly 1,600 dealers were lost.

Yet, some dealerships have existed for well over 100 years. John Smith Co. of Smyrna, Ga., a Chevrolet and Geo dealer, began as a carriage maker in 1869. Swab Wagon Co. of Elizabethville, Pa., also built wagons as far back as 1868. The dealership has sold Saxon, Chevrolet, Studebaker, Packard, Mercedes-Benz, Avanti II, and now sells Chryslers, Plymouths, and Dodges.[9]

Front wheel drive was not new to America, even though auto makers often made it sound like an invention of the late 1970s and 1980s. The Front-Drive automobile, seen here, was introduced in 1907. This prototype was run as fast as 30 mph, a respectable speed for the time.

But the contest for luxury car production leadership was resting between two very American makes: Lincoln and Cadillac. There had been a giant gap in production figures between the makes. For example, the 1 millionth Lincoln was made on March 25, 1968. However, Cadillac made its 6 millionth car on February 7, 1977. Lincoln had a lot of catching up to do. For 1988, Lincoln outproduced Cadillac for the first time, 280,659 to 270,844. It was a substantial drop from Cadillac's record high in 1976 of 309,139 sales. Riding the crest of Lincoln popularity was the Town Car, which had begun modestly in 1981 with 32,839 units (including the Town Coupe). For 1988 production on the Town Car, alone was 128,533. What tripped up Cadillac and gave rise to Lincoln was Cadillac's downsizing (in 1985 it went from a wheelbase of 121.5 inches to 110.8 and for 1986 the Eldorado and Seville shortened from 114 inches to 108) and its introduction of ill-

Lee Iacocca promoted Lincoln's rise when he worked at Ford.

fated innovations such as the 8-6-4 V-8. A conservative image for luxury and quality had finally stuck to Lincoln, and buyers who liked large cars almost stood in line at Lincoln dealerships. They felt Cadillac had abandoned them. With Lincoln's image gaining stability, the cars retained higher value. This, too, pleased buyers and made Lincoln one of the few domestic success stories of the 1980s.

It took more than six decades, but Henry Ford's plan had worked. When he took over Lincoln from Henry and Wilfred Leland, Ford wanted a price leader to add prestige to his low-price line. It was the might of the Ford Motor Company that kept Lincoln afloat during lean sales periods, just as the might of General Motors had saved Cadillac.

What was to be a new Thunderbird design became the Lincoln Continental of 1961 through the influence of Robert S. McNamara, a Ford Whiz Kid (one of a group of highly promising executives who gave vitality to the company under Henry Ford II). The public liked the car's so-called suicide doors and classic styling. The new model put Lincoln closer in sync with public taste. While with Ford, Lee Iacocca also promoted the rise of Lincoln. But the make still had a weaker image compared to Cadillac and thus failed to meet the needs of many buyers. This key element for success was missing.

The horsepower race with big, brawny V-8s of the late 1960s and 1970s recalled the days of massive precision engines that powered the legendary Duesenbergs. In 1928 a Model J was run on the Indianapolis Speedway at an honest 89 mph in second gear and 116 in high. The Duesenberg catalog claimed that even at 100 mph the engine was not overtaxed. In literature, the factory claimed 129 mph in supercharged version for a convertible coupe. The actual horsepower rating of 265 is believed possible. The Duesenberg Model J delivered about twice the horsepower of most other cars in its day.[10] An extravagantly expensive car, it gained much appreciation among the newly rich, such as movie stars. "Old money" luxury car buyers who had become accustomed to their wealth often chose quiet, stately, conservative cars. Hence, Packards, Pierce-Arrows, and Peerless automobiles sold better in the eastern states where many of established wealth had settled. It was not uncommon for a price of $15,000 or more to be tagged to a finished Duesenberg in the 1930s, with custom body and special-order appointments!

When the muscle car craze began with the Pontiac GTO, massive power was being boosted out of standard engines. For 1964 the GTO option cost $296 for any LeMans model. By raising horsepower on a car with a light body and modest chassis more power was being delivered in the medium price range than the Duesenberg ever had. For 1968, with John DeLorean at the helm, Pontiac issued its 428 cid V-8, and by 1971 a massive 455 cid engine with four-barrel carburetor (on the Grand Prix) made for blistering performance. The 455 in the 1971 GTO boasted 335 hp at 4800 rpm with a compression ratio of 8.4 to 1. For 1981, Pontiac's turbo-charged 301 cid V-8 was still a performer, doing zero to 60 mph in 8.2 seconds. In 1984 a special competition kit with spoilers, flares, deflectors, and more, took a Twin Turbo GTO Trans Am to a verified 204 mph! The new cars may not have the status and appeal of a true classic car from the 1930s, but when it comes to performance, Duesenberg, eat your heart out!

During auto shows in 1988, Lincoln's Machete was one of numerous concept cars auto makers produced for the show circuit.

Large gave way to small in the aftermath of the gas crunch which hit America in the 1970s. Late in that decade the 460 and 400 cubic inch engines had been sacrificed. The Mark VII bowed for 1984 and picked up the grand tradition of the 1960s. Its 302 cubic inch engine for 1985 added top performance to the neo-classic package. High-tech features were plentiful on the 1995 Continental which was viewed by company officials as the car which would launch Lincoln into the next century—and continue to make the marque the competitor its pioneers had hoped it would be![6]

The American car buyer had changed tastes in options, too. In 1950 just over 33 percent of all new American cars had automatic transmissions. For 1977 that had jumped to 95.2 percent. But for 1980 it dropped to 82.7 percent.

In 1955 only 1.5 percent of new cars had factory air conditioning. For 1967 that had risen to 38 percent, and for 1977 was almost 82 percent. In 1980, this slipped to 73 percent. Disc brakes, which had been on only four percent of new cars in 1966 was up to 100 percent for 1977, 1978, and 1979. This dipped to 82 percent for 1980. There were drops in the number of cars with power steering in the early 1980s, and a preference for radial steel belted tires was pronounced in that decade, also

Ford boldly showed the press this minivan concept vehicle with substantial fanfare. A turntable usually rotated the van so that spectators at shows could give maximum attention to the features.

High costs and changes in public demand changed the professional car field, an offshoot of the automobile industry. Hard hit by recessions and financial stress in the 1980s, the professional car field was ripe with talks of merger, failures, and corporate reshuffling. Superior, Sayers & Scoville, Miller-Meteor, Hess & Eisenhardt, and several other makers of custom-ordered limousines, hearses, ambulances, and flower cars had proud histories in the handmade production of their vehicles. For decades stock chassis from Cadillac, Lincoln, Buick, Pontiac, Pierce-Arrow, Packard, and others from were shipped from factories to the professional car plants for conversion. Sectioning, enhanced body parts, heavy-duty suspensions, and other updates were made. It was not uncommon for a special-ordered hearse or ambulance in the early 1970s to sell for $10,000, and that was for a medium-priced Oldsmobile chassis! In the 1980s this cost had tripled. Businesses which wanted such vehicles were less and less able to afford them. Time-intensive high production costs didn't help the makers, either. And smaller but aggressive companies—such as Armbruster-Stageway—were cutting into established markets. The 1980s were a far cry from the early days.

Among car makers still active in the American automobile

The five-point formula for success first was applied in the professional car field with the mass production of commercially built hearses and ambulances in 1909. While the first recorded use of an ambulance took place years before and involved a Woods Electric in 1900 in New York City (it only went 9 mph and its toughest challenge was not getting blocked in by streets which were congested with horses and carriages), the reliability of motor vehicles as emergency vehicles and funeral coaches was still questionable until 1909. The industry-within-an-industry would continue to grow with the advancement of the automobile industry. In the late 1940s the trade witnessed phenomenal production levels, with such makers as Henney prominent in the field. But the 1950s would begin a series of downturns culminating with disaster for some companies. The 1980s were even worse.

Pontiac was not left out of the concept car competition. The GM division often poured much money into presenting its ideas to the world.

industry, AMC struggled through most of its years. For 1971 it made only 2.75 percent of all new cars in the country. This jumped to 3.16 percent for 1972, but AMC made only 279,132 vehicles. In 1972 General Motors led the car makers with more than 54 percent of the market. Ford claimed a little more than 27 percent. Chrysler was just shy of 15.5 percent.

In the last 20 years of the American auto industry's first century, corporate shuffling of personnel in divisions, realignment of plants and work forces, leasing programs, and cautious moves in corporate directions had become common techniques for survival. Styling trends after 1980 favored small cars with aerodynamic treatments along a wedge principle for least resistance. Recreational vehicles gained in popularity and the rise of the van and minivan took place, which offered boxy comfort with enhanced cargo-carrying versatility in what appeared to be a replacement for the once popular family station wagon. Styling turned as never before toward the once-utilitarian pickup truck in the 1990s as demand for sporty trucks with extra seating and luxuries increased.

Adding to the construction cost and weight of cars, while sapping horsepower, was an array of government-stipulated

The dash area of a 1996 Oldsmobile hardly resembled the dash of a century before. In the 1990s "mission statements" had become a trendy way for companies to state their purpose. Oldsmobile's Centennial Plan was summarized in its mission statement: "The Oldsmobile team will work together to earn and keep its customers by providing internationally-focused vehicles and uncompromised satisfaction throughout the shopping, buying and ownership experience."

Oldsmobile wasted no time in announcing its anniversary when the 1996 cars were introduced. "On August 21, 1997, Oldsmobile will be the first American automobile maker to celebrate its 100th birthday. By then, a very different car company will be in place, an organization that is far stronger and more dynamic in its response to competitive challenge," said a news release. Oldsmobile had come a long way since the days of Ransom E. Olds!

In the early 1990s, drive-in movie theaters became a rarity. Often falling into disrepair and not being able to compete with the sophisticated visual and audible advances maximized by inside movie theaters, most drive-ins were leveled. Their land was developed into shopping centers or malls. The face of Route 66 had drastically changed with the rise of superhighways. So did a cherished way of life.

"improvements." Engine emissions were controlled with strong regulations beginning in 1973 and 1974, low-impact bumpers were mandated, and eventually mileage standards and a host of other guidelines were legislated for the industry. At times during the 1970s and 1990s, the American auto industry seemed to be demoralized.

Was the vision of the early automotive pioneers gone forever? There were a few visionaries who came to industry-wide significance in the 1980s and 1990s. Their excitement for the automobile in America and what the industry could accomplish were encouragements amid a stormy sea of uncertainty. Among the few were engineer John DeLorean who traced his automotive background to Chrysler, Packard, Pontiac, and Chevrolet and eventually targeted America with his foreign-made, rear-engined, stainless-steel bodied DeLorean sports car for 1982. But pushed to the wall to succeed, he gave in to illegal tactics for financial support. There was Lee Iacocca who had bridled the imagination of America with the Mustang, later moved to Chrysler where he introduced the minivan and other new ventures, and became, to some, a modern day manifestation of Walter P. Chrysler and the corporation's champion. When Iacocca started with Ford in 1948 his week's pay was $37.40. In 1986 he had come a long way: His annual salary, bonus, and stock options amounted to $20.5 million. *Business Week* reserved the cover of one issue for Iacocca who, it claimed, was the highest paid executive in the United States!

GM's launch of Saturn as a marque and the setting up of its dealer network beginning in 1985, made from scratch and according to stringent principles, was a bold move. The Saturn was aimed against Honda, Mazda, and Nissan, among others. Reorganization at Ford brought the company from its onrush toward disaster and made it a trend-setter in management and production. The absorption of AMC by Chrysler saved the AMC dealer network, gave Chrysler more market strength with Jeep, and probably was inevitable. By 1990, corporate mentality ruled the industry and gaining in significance were special consultants, market studies, government guidelines to save the environment, cautious business maneuvers, and work patterns adapted from the Japanese. It was a business trend which echoed throughout America.

Occasionally experiments with alternate fuel sources, such as electricity, still intrigued the industry as it sought a low-cost fuel option amid projections of diminishing oil reserves. Had Thomas Edison lived to the present, the interest in electric cars near the end of the 20th century would have made him say, "I told you so."

Anniversaries were reached by the auto makers. Oldsmobile as a make, preceding the formation of the company, reached its 100th year in 1996. Cadillac reached its 90th in 1992. Ford, under its present corporate manifestation, reached its 90th year in 1993. Chevrolet made it to its 80th year in 1991. Dodge reached age 80 in 1994. Chrysler reached its 70th year as a make in 1994.

These anniversaries, notable as they were, received modest promotion. Public enthusiasm for the milestones seemed practically nonexistent. Except for some vague references in occasional feature stories in tabloids and except for a few special events, the anniversaries were used mainly as sales tools in ad campaigns.

Was there a fear that these milestones in age stereotyped the American car makers as "senior citizens," with all the drawbacks that term implied? Was age being played down?

If so, then who carries the torch for the rich heritage of the American automobile and who waves the banner for the industry which it spawned?

The Y-Job for 1938 was GM's first serious effort to field a dream car for public viewing. The car predicted future styling trends, especially for Buick.

Notes

1. An enlightening treatment of the VW is offered by Terry Shuler with Griffith Borgeson and Jerry Sloniger in *The Origin of the VW Beetle,* Automobile Quarterly Publications, Kutztown, Pa., 1985. Observations about the Beetle are derived from this book plus factory literature in the author's collection.

2. *The American Cyclecar,* Charles P. Root & Co., Chicago, Vol. 1, No. 7, for May 1914.

3. Ibid., page 18; the Cyclecar Association of America, which was barely a half year old in May 1914, had limited cyclecar reliability competition to vehicles of 125 hp and with a maximum weight not more than 1,150 lbs. Cyclecars were able to climb rough terrain unlike most other normal size cars mainly due to their lesser weight and extremely low point of gravity. They also offered very economical upkeep, miserly gas mileage, and were stingy on oil usage compared to most other American makes of the time. These features were to mark many of the small import cars which sold successfully in America in the 1970s. Other popular cyclecars included Merz, Woods Mobilette, Flagler, Steco, Trumbull, Pioneer, Rayfield, and Coey Junior.

4. *Ward's Automotive Yearbook 1981,* Ward's Communications, Inc., Detroit, 1981; pg. 23.

5. Ibid., pg. 69.

6. Information gleaned from *Automotive News Yearbook* for 1989, and *Lincoln, 1945-1995,* Gregory Von Dare, Motorbooks International, Osceola, Wis., 1995.

7. *The Auto Review,* Automobile Club of St. Louis, St. Louis, Mo., July 1906, pg. 37.

8. Information based on recent interviews conducted by this author.

9. *Automotive News,* Crain Communications, Detroit, Feb. 13, 1984, page 1; and January 27, 1992, page 1. Details about the Smith and Swab dealerships come from *SAH Journal,* issue 159, Nov.-Dec. 1995, Samuel V. Fiorani, editor; Society of Automotive Historians, P.O. Box 7073, St. Daniels, Pa. 19087-7073; pg. 6.

10. *Duesenberg, The Pursuit of Perfection,* Fred Roe, Dalton Watson, London; 1982, 1986; pp. 187-188.

12
DU-J14

Chapter 9

Who Carries the Torch?

Surviving companies in the American auto industry were revitalized in the late 1980s and early 1990s, moving vigorously ahead into the industry's second century. Many lessons for success were learned in the first 100 years. Many were forgotten. Unless history is kept alive, many mistakes will be repeated. True, the industry is still making history. But the antique car hobby is preserving it.

What interest is it to General Motors to preserve the histories of Templar? Peerless? Durant? Locomobile? Why should Chrysler executives care about maintaining knowledge of Roamer, Royal Electric, Sampson, or Saxon? Do Ford officials really wish to spend their time keeping up with the past accomplishments of Kaiser, Tucker, the Lane Steamer, or Haynes?

Logically, they don't. At least, not in most practical applications regarding their daily work. So when it comes to carrying the torch of history for the entire auto industry, it is up to hobbyists.

By 1958 there were 11,000 antique cars dating back to the 1800s that had been spared by collectors. Some of the owners restored and babied their acquisitions as best they could. Some merely preserved what was there in hopes that missing parts, proper tires, and necessary information would one day come to light and enable them to complete the restoration. With increased fervor beginning in the 1960s the collector car hobby

Opposite, above: Around 1900, car hobbyists were called "Automobilists." They gathered with common interests in motoring and put their cars to the test in hill climbing and cross country events.

Opposite, below: By 1920, car hobbyists who harkened to the call of the open road had been influential in lobbying governmental officials for more and better roads. This, in turn, brought cities closer together in commerce.

By World War II, hobbyists had turned toward antique cars. The "old timers," as the cars usually were called, reminded collectors of bygone days and how America's history was reflected in many different wheels that had been in motion, such as this International highwheeler.

became big business. Tire makers resurrected old molds to manufacture obsolete tire patterns. Industrious collectors and speculators scavenged old dealerships for obsolete mechanical and trim parts, plus sales and technical catalogs. Former upholstery materials were remade. Restoration shops increased in number. Major swap meets and antique car shows abounded. The automobile industry in America had spawned yet another industry.[1]

The movement for car owners to be involved in clubs dates to the early years of the 20th century. "The American Motor League is a national organization of automobilists," wrote President I. B. Potter in the October edition of *MoToR*. "It represents the first systematic and successful attempt to organize the users, makers, dealers, and friends of the motor car into a strong and useful body. Its increase in numbers and growth in popular favor give substantial proof that its mission is appreciated." He noted that in January 1903 "less than four percent of the users of motor cars in this country were members of any organization whatsoever." His group existed to organize motorists and to promote the installation of road signs

Lovingly restored by patient hobbyists, cars like this rare 1939 LaSalle convertible sedan make a hit with spectators as entries in parades and at civic events. Every antique car that enters such an event alerts the public to America's rich automotive tradition.

(especially for safety), "lead and direct the agitation for better roads," and "prepare maps and descriptions of all local routes." Half a century later, hobby clubs were doing similar jobs. They united members in common causes. They stood in support or opposition to governmental regulations for motoring. They offered tour events and technical help for their members.

The American Automobile Association (AAA) was headed by President Julian A. Chase in 1903. In the same issue of *MoToR*, he noted how the automobile "while occupying the field of sport and recreation. . . has now gone on the list of necessities" and that the AAA was following this trend. Until then, the organization had been devoted to sport and recreational uses of cars. The "Three A's" (as it was called then) changed its constitution and bylaws to get in step with the new direction. Organized in 1902 through the combining of nearly all major clubs in large cities, it had become a dominating force in establishing and monitoring racing, a sport that many owners of early cars loved to pursue. AAA brought standards to the events and emphasized safety. The "Good Roads Movement" was a prime target for the AAA.

By 1960 many states had legislated the use of special license plates and designations for antique vehicles. In California a car had to be over 35 years old and the owner had to pay a regular fee plus $2. In Connecticut, owners of cars built before 1926 paid the regular fee plus $5 for as long as the owner kept the car. A special enameled plate was issued, which itself has become collectible. In Florida a car had to be over 25 years old, owners paid a minimum fee of $5, and the state police had to inspect the car annually. Michigan made it easy: owners of cars made before 1926 paid $6 for as long as they owned the car. Nebraska had a similar law but the cost was $5 and cars had to be over 40. Ohio charged $10 for the life of the car if it was over 35 years old. Hobbyists in Oregon enjoyed their regulation: cars over 25 years old were charged only $1 annually!

Cars of note are preserved due to the public interest in old cars and a healthy hobby following. This Lincoln, specially built for the use of the Royal Family of England, has been on display many years in Dearborn, at the Henry Ford Museum.

Over subsequent years interest in obsolete cars increased. In the 1930s pockets of old car hobbyists began banding together to meet mutual needs and foster fellowship in ways the AAA or other clubs initially had done decades before. But while AAA concentrated on newer cars and especially wanted to serve their drivers, hobbyists were gathering under the banner of historical preservation and restoration.

The earliest national hobby club to form was the Antique Automobile Club of America (AACA) in 1935. Philadelphia was the location. By 1958 there were more than 6,000 members in the AACA. The club co-sponsored the new national Glidden Tours, which were week-long events covering several states. Regional clubs, a national publication, and a major swap meet in Hershey, Pa., were notable achievements of the club. The Hershey Fall Meet became the apex of annual hobby activities, and continues to this day.

The Horseless Carriage Club of America (HCCA) originated as the Horseless Carriage Club of Los Angeles in 1937. It emphasized ownership of brass era cars made before 1916 and retained this designation for voting membership. It, too,

This Selden car, built according to the patent designs of George Selden, was used in the legal case between Selden and Henry Ford. On display for the public, it enlightens the present generations to America's automotive history.

fostered regional groups, offered a publication, and generated club projects.

In 1939 the Veteran Motor Car Club of America (VMCCA) was formed and was predominate in New England. It co-sponsored the Glidden Tours with the AACA in alternating years and early on was similar to the AACA in structure and benefits to the hobbyist. Interestingly, one of the 12 founders of the VMCCA was M. J. "Jerry" Duryea, son of Charles E. Duryea, one of America's first automotive pioneers.

The VMCCA, AACA, and HCCA each sponsored gymkhanas, runs, hill club competitions, and social events. And each grew in membership.

In the 1940s the antique car hobby was in its natal stage. With few car manufacturers in existence hobbyists realized that many makes and the industrial achievements of their designers would be forgotten unless an effort was made to preserve this heritage. Even the auto makers who were still in operation did not take as much interest in preserving their own histories as did hobbyists. It was the antique car hobbyist who began to carry the torch of history for the American automobile industry.

In May 1944, the editor of *The Horseless Carriage Club Gazette*

At least 50 private and public museums plus various large collections featuring antique automobiles were formed prior to 1965. They served as a reference source for restorers who wanted to see how a similar car to theirs was put together before they started a restoration. The museums also served as a source for cars as the collections were thinned or as museums went out of business.

The McIntyre highwheeler, of Auburn, Ind., is one of numerous cars made in that state and which are on display in the A-C-D Museum. Regional museums often specialize in collecting cars of their area. This, too, enriches our understanding of history and perpetuates the torch-carrying aspects of car collecting.

printed this letter from Ransom E. Olds: "I notice. . . you show an Oldsmobile of 1902. This should be 1900, as that is the year I got out these samples which did not have fenders. In 1901 I built 400 that were fitted with fenders. In 1902 the production was nearly 4,000 at which time I used wood wheels mostly. I am writing you so that in any future publications you can use the above figures."[2]

Olds had become an honorary member of the Horseless Carriage Club, which saluted him as a pioneer. By comments like this he gave credibility to the realization that clubs and their members were now carrying the torch. Existing auto makers were parochial in present-day endeavors and often concentrated on sales, not history. But with hobby clubs there was a seriousness in historical preservation and an intensity in uncovering the past as accurately as possible. This would benefit the industry and car makers when anniversaries arose and vintage cars were needed for display. Old cars sometimes were used for advertisements, too. By the 1990s, new car shows in major cities across America often invited a display of vintage vehicles from local clubs as historical seasoning for the events!

Other automotive pioneers who had been corporate big wheels in the industry became active in local and national clubs.

Unique in its collection of race cars and memorabilia is the museum of the Indianapolis Motor Speedway.

Famous and vintage race cars are pleasantly displayed for public viewing and have been for many years. With the continued high interest in the annual 500 mile race, many visitors who attend the event stop by the museum.

George P. Dorris was one of five founders of the Horseless Carriage Club of Missouri, Inc., in December of 1944 and soon got his friend A. L. Dyke, another pioneer, active in the club. The club became an associate with the Horseless Carriage Club

Among the notable car museum locations prior to 1965 were James Melton's Autorama in Hypoluxo, Fla., which had its beginning in the popular singer's collector efforts, which dated to the 1930s. The Cameron Peck collection in Chicago and the Barney Pollard collection in Detroit were well known. Henry Austin Clark, an extremely helpful and generous collector, took pride in his Long Island Automotive Museum, which by 1959 held about 100 cars. The transportation display at the Henry Ford Museum had about 175 cars, ranging from an 1865 Roper Steam Carriage to cars from the 1930s. It remains a natural magnet for early hobbyists. The Museum of Science and Industry in Chicago featured a fine display of cars dating to an 1893 Bernardi and an 1896 Benz. The Chicago museum also commemorated the 50th anniversary of the first auto race in America with a special display that opened on November 2, 1945, and featured various events culminating in a run by early cars over the original 1895 course on Thanksgiving Day. William E. Swigart, Jr., who had been president of the AACA, had his own museum in Huntingdon, Pa., featuring about 40 cars, including a 1901 Winton and a collection of brass lamps, radiator caps, and much automobilia. Harold Warp ran his Pioneer Village in Minden, Neb., which filled 12 buildings and featured antique cars.

George P. Dorris, seen here at the wheel of a vintage St. Louis at a car show in the late 1940s, is joined by A. L. Dyke. Both were automotive pioneers and were active as hobbyists well into the 1960s.

of Los Angeles and was credited as the first region of the HCCA. In the late 1940s and early 1950s the two pioneers-turned-hobbyists were featured by newspapers and magazines in cross-country drives in a 1902 St. Louis Boston Model that had been engineered by Dorris. He had purchased the car from Art Twohy in California, a national figure in the HCCA. When Dorris and Dyke made their trips, it wasn't the automobile industry that promoted them; it was hobby clubs. Yet, their activities reflected on the early years of the American automobile industry. The torch had been passed.

Dyke witnessed the growing demand for technical literature among collectors and helped numerous hobbyists nationwide in ways most companies in the auto industry could not; some chose not to take the time. His system for loaning was simple: "He would place a value on the piece requested by a borrower and ask that person to write a check for the amount. Dyke held the check until the piece was returned, then handed back the check. He boasted that with this system, he never lost a piece in his collection!"[3] Eventually, he gave this extensive collection of

Who knows how many young children had their first experience of seeing an air-cooled Franklin by coming to a museum?

documents to the automotive literature section at the Detroit Public Library. It was yet another example of a hobbyist rather than the auto industry helping to preserve the past.

Car makers over the years preserved what was advantageous for the present sale of cars. Few kept reference material such as Dyke. Many of the companies were helpful in answering historical inquiries, to a point. But if the request was costly or time-consuming, it was not mainstream to the corporate mind-set.

By 1960 it was estimated that more than 100,000 people had an interest in the old car hobby and America's automotive heritage. Other clubs that centered on particular marques had been formed. Among them were the Auburn-Cord-Duesenberg Club, Classic Car Club of America, Curved Dash Olds Club, H. H. Franklin Club, Haynes-Apperson Owners Club, Model A Restorers Club, Model T Club, Steam Owners Club, and Packard Automobile Classics. Other clubs that fostered foreign makes also existed, such as the Rolls-Royce Club and the Mercedes-Benz Club of America.

The AACA, HCCA, and VMCCA saluted older cars as central to the hobby—such as a 1902 Holsman, 1903

Prior to 1965, Powers Auto Museum, Southington, Conn., had 65 cars from 1896 to 1932 on display. In St. Louis, Lowell Frei's museum had about 50 cars on view in a converted dairy building, with another 50 he rotated into the display. The Museum of Antique Autos in Princeton, Mass., had about 200 cars on display. Sixty cars from 1898 to 1934 were housed at Upstate Auto Museum, Bridgewater, N.Y. Of course, the Smithsonian had its collection of cars, Horn's Cars of Yesterday was in operation in Sarasota, Fla., and the Indianapolis Speedway Museum was drawing big crowds. Also bringing the heritage of America's automotive past on a regional basis were Waco's in Miami, Protsman's in Atlanta, Burd's in Cedar Falls, Iowa, Poll's in Holland, Mich., Kelsey's in Camdenton, Mo., Pollock's in Pottstown, Pa., the Horseless Carriage Museum in Rapid City, S.D., the Car and Carriage Caravan in Luray, Va., and the Sunflower Museum, Lake Tomahawk, Wis. February of 1962 marked the opening of Harrah's in Reno, Nev. In 1965 it displayed 300 antique, classic, and vintage motor cars, the 1908 Thomas Flyer, winner of the New York to Paris Race in 1908, as the cornerstone. In 1970 Harrah's had its 1 millionth visitor! Museums have been a high-visibility way for the heritage of America's automobile industry to be promoted to the public at large, introducing new generations to our automotive past.

How many middle-age adults stood in front of this Duesenberg, marking their first confrontation with the famous marque?

Oldsmobile, 1905 Knox, 1909 Buick, or 1910 White steam car. Cars up to about 1920 were encouraged to appear at events, although they were not held in high regard, as were older cars.

By 1960 many states recognized the lobbying force of the growing hobby and issued license plates for vintage vehicles. But the term "antique" was being applied to cars that ranged from 25 to 40 years old, depending on the state.

The American automobile of the past became classified and appreciated like never before, thanks to clubs. Clubs categorized cars along historical lines: brass cars, veterans, vintage cars, classics, and special interest cars. Such terms had a bearing on the way in which the general public viewed the advances of the automobile industry itself. It even has influenced modern car development and advertising, as recent car makers design and promote new cars with an eye to the great automobiles of the past.

The classic category as determined by the AACA initially included the Auburn 8 and V-12, the V-12 and V-16 Cadillac, Cord, Cunningham, Duesenberg, du Pont, Franklin, LaSalle, the V-8 and V-12 Lincoln phaeton or other models with special coachwork, and the Locomobile (excluding the Junior 8 and models with Lycoming engines). In 1957 the category was expanded to include the V-16 Marmon, Packard (except for the 110 and 120 models), Pierce-Arrow, Rolls-Royce models made in Springfield, Mass., Ruxton, and Stutz. The Classic Car Club of America developed the list even more.

The torch was being carried by hobbyists as never before. New generations of Americans were introduced to such nearly forgotten makes as Jewett, Moyer, Owen Magnetic, Wills St.

The Auburn-Cord-Duesenberg Museum in Auburn, Ind., is an example of how an important and historic building that was connected with car manufacturing can successfully be renovated into an outstanding museum location.

Some museums also served as points of sale, such as this now dispersed collection once housed in Kansas City's Union Station.

The Henry Ford Museum and Greenfield Museum in Dearborn, Mich., are popular magnets that attract old car collectors. Swap meets at numerous locations such as Hershey and Carlisle, Pa., and Iola, Wis., also offer the public massive car shows. (Photo by M. Lawrence Hassel)

What countless number of octogenarians have viewed cars like this Haynes and have recalled stories from their youth?

Clair, Playboy, Rickenbacker, Roosevelt, Sears, Simplo, Templar, Velie, and Wolverine. Even rare or ancient trucks such as Hug and the high-wheeled International Harvester were rediscovered. The exploits of automotive pioneers were researched and put in print. More and more hobby magazines and books were printed with increasing circulation.

Even more recent auto executives saw value in the hobby. Dick Teague, who spearheaded the design efforts of AMC through some of its best product years and who had also designed for Packard, was an active hobbyist for most of his life. He learned from the past and applied that knowledge to the future. Brooks Stevens, a famous designer who breathed excitement into the Studebaker Gran Turismo Hawk and Wagonaire in the 1960s, among numerous other automotive credits, also was appreciative of hobby activities. More than a few executives in the American automobile industry became active in one form or another in the hobby. By studying history, the industry could rediscover past innovations that become feasible for production due to technological advancements in manufacturing. History also helped current auto planners avoid former pitfalls.

As the historical wheels are kept in motion with every restored car that takes on new life, so the hobby carries the torch for other aspects of the auto industry. Hobbyists preserve dealer histories, service station paraphernalia, vintage automotive garments, original artwork for ads and promotions, and factory files. The material that has been preserved privately is on a scale that taxes the mind. Tens of thousands of artifacts and documents, properly identified and appreciated, are pieces to the puzzle picture of the auto industry's first century.

The hobby has become a business for many. Auction companies have their hectic schedules. Weekend parts vendors, hoping to pay for their hobby, have planned their swap circuits months in advance. Speculators will always be around.

It has put a price on history.

In 1906, *MoToR* advertised the sale of used cars. "White, 1903 model; new engine and generator; car in perfect order; price, $700, or exchange for 1905 Franklin runabout," said one ad from New York City. An ad from Washington, D.C., told of a Thomas Model 18 tonneau with Solar headlight for $350. From Buffalo, N.Y., a Winton Model C in perfect condition was selling for $1,250. Those prices, even with an inflation factor, rose much higher than the original values due to the hobby. The same came true for other vintages. In 1950, a 1931 Stutz convertible coupe, which originally had sold new for about $3,600, could be bought for $50. By 1995 that same car, fully restored, was valued in top condition at $80,000! Auction prices for the same car were hard pressed to reach even half that figure in the late 1970s. What price can be put on history?

Newspapers have hyped high prices paid for classic cars in the 1980s and 1990s. When the million-dollar mark is reached at an old car auction, it is news. Such information has falsely tainted the public's image of the hobby as merely a speculation sport. What price can be put on the hobby?

Automobilia also has increased in value. What may appear to be trash often contains automotive treasures. A Pontiac Service Craftsman mechanic's pin from the 1930s was priced at $40 in the early 1990s. A Ford cigarette lighter from the 1950s may go for $25. Even a MoPar silicone auto cleaner tin can from the 1960s can be priced at $20. An Illinois soybean license plate from 1943 can carry a tag of $30. A Firestone Tires porcelain sign can sell for $125. Model cars and pedal cars often have taken astronomical rises in values. What price can be put on history?[4]

Collectability has placed an invisible dollar sign in front of almost every type of antiquated automotive gadget there is. The saving grace is that such dollar signs will help preserve historical items for the future.

More important than any price applied to the antique car

Car hobbyists who maintain vehicles like this 1950 Cadillac bring a museum-like experience to the out-of-doors and prove that cars of the past were built to last.

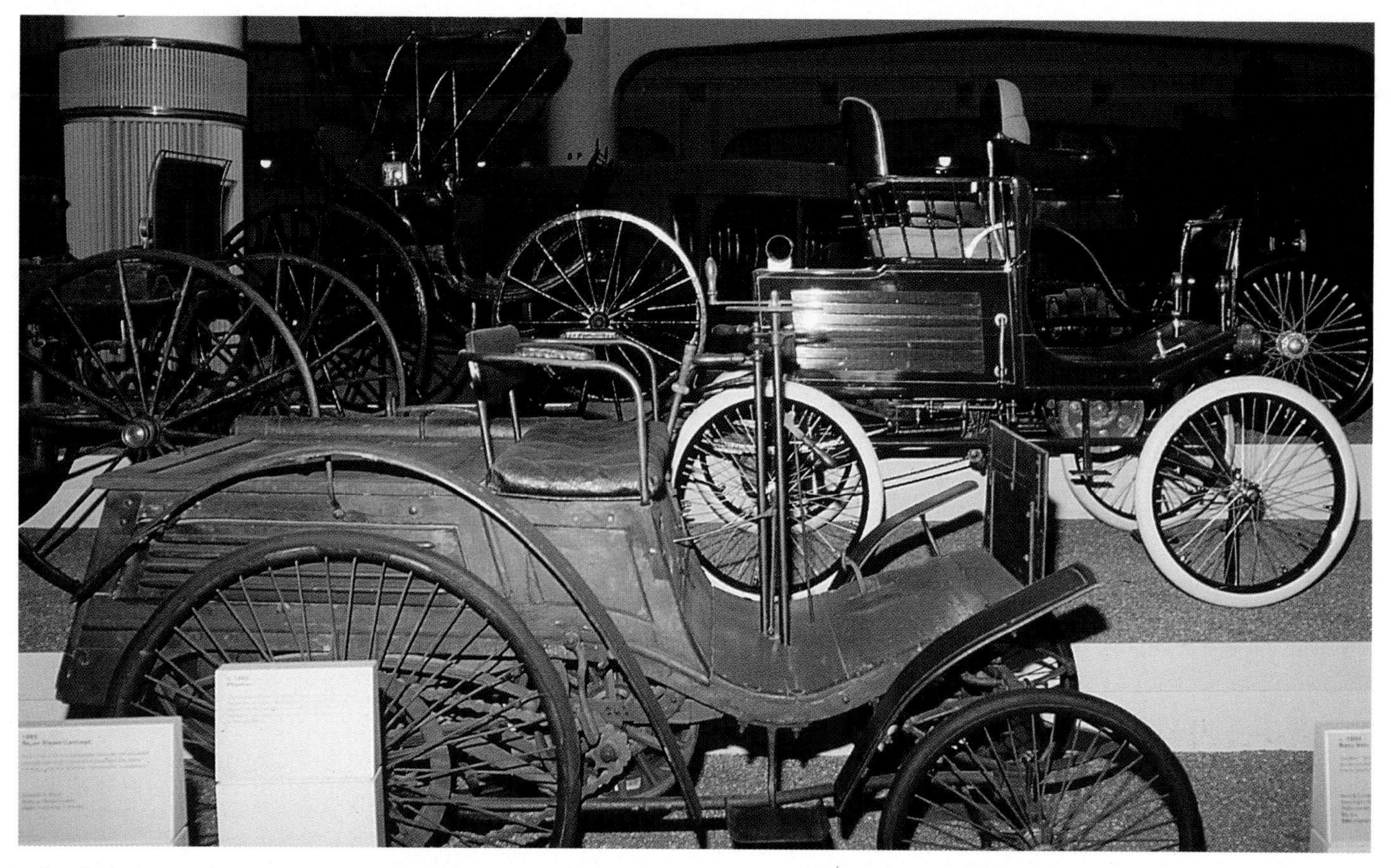

The wheels that put this nation in motion are vivid reminders of the past. Had it not been for such vehicles, America would not have developed like it did and most likely would not have risen to such world importance.

Presidents gave up their horse-drawn carriages for cars. The American automobile and the advancement of society have walked together for a century, hand in hand.

The pioneers who kept America on wheels played a vital part in furthering our goals and national image.

In makes that at one time were powerhouses in the industry but have faded into history, the story of America is reflected.

hobby is the matter of value. Even more than the industry itself, old car hobbyists value the past, value the advancements and traditions of the industry's first century. In that appreciation is greatness that can be used to benefit the present and the future. Yes, there is tremendous value in the hobby.

The history of the industry will not be preserved by the few auto makers still in business. It is up to each hobbyist.

Above every price tag on any vintage car, obsolete sign, or old automotive magazine looms the heritage of the industry—and of every American. And bringing light to the industry itself is the antique automobile hobby, the torch bearer of a rich and rewarding heritage!

Reflected in every collector car, every vintage vehicle, is the torch of a nation's heritage, held before the eyes of the world by the hand of the hobbyist!

Notes

1. *Buy an Antique Car*, a handbook for those interested in the world's most fascinating hobby, by Scott and Margaret Bailey, Floyd Clymer Publications, Los Angeles, Calif., 1958; p. 9 ff. Certain information on car clubs appearing later in the text also comes from this source.
2. *The Horseless Carriage Club Gazette*, Horseless Carriage Club of Los Angeles, Vol. 6, No. 1, May 15, 1944; pp. 3 & 9.
3. *50 years of Rigs that Run, the Golden Anniversary history of the Horseless Carriage Club of Missouri, Inc.*, by Gerald Perschbacher, published by the HCCM, St. Louis, Mo., 1994; p. 7. Even Don Selden, a car salesman and the nephew of patent mogul George B. Selden, became a hobbyist in 1944.
4. *American Automobilia*, an illustrated history and price guide, by Jim and Nancy Schaut, Wallace-Homestead Book Company, Radnor, Pa., 1994; pp. 11, 14, 16, and 71.
5. *The Horseless Carriage Club Gazette*, June 1945, p. 7.

J. Frank Duryea of Madison, Conn., who with his brother had been credited with building the first successful gasoline automobile in America, also was supportive of hobby interests. On April 22, 1945, he spoke before the Horseless Carriage Club of Los Angeles at the L.A. County Museum. He told of his pioneer efforts and those of the earliest pioneers such as Daimler and the founding of the Stevens-Duryea Automobile Company. Club president George Shafer told the audience, "This occasion is something for you, your children, and your children's children to remember."[5]

American Vehicle Club List

Compiled by Chad Elmore, *Old Cars Weekly News & Marketplace*

GENERAL INTEREST

American Station Wagon Owners Assoc., 6110 Bethesda Way, Indianapolis, IN 46254-5060. Kenneth C. McDaniel, (317)291-0321.

American Truck Historical Society (ATHS), P.O. Box 531168 Birmingham, AL 35253-1168. (300 Office Park Drive, Suite #120, Birmingham, AL 35223). Larry L. Scheef, (205)870-0566. http//www.the-matrix.com/aths/truck/htm/

Antique Automobile Club of America (AACA), 501 W. Governor Rd., P.O. Box 417, Hershey, PA 17033. (717)534-1910.

Antique Truck Club of America (ATCA), P.O. Box 291, Hershey, PA 17033.

Classic Car Club Of America (CCCA), 1645 Des Plaines River Rd. #7, Des Plaines, IL 60018. (708)390-0443, fax (708)390-7118.

Classic Car Club Of America – Classic Car Club of America Museum, 6865 Hickory Corners, Hickory Corners, MI 49060. Tom Kayser, (616)671-5089.

Contemporary Historical Vehicle Assoc., P.O. Box 98, Tecumseh, KS 66542-0098. Mary Jean Flory, (913)233-6715.

Fifties Automobile Club of America, 1114 Furman Dr., Egg Harbor Township, NJ 08234. William Schmoll, (609)927-4967.

Horseless Carriage Club of America (HCCA), 128 S. Cypress St., Orange, CA 92666-1314. (714)538-4222.

International Society for Vehicle Preservation, P.O. Box 50046, Tucson, AZ 85703-1046. (602)622-2201.

Microcar and Minicar Club, P.O. Box 43137, Upper Montclair, NJ 07043.

Mid-America Old-Time Automobile Assoc., 8 Jones Ln., Morrilton, AR 72110. Buddy Hoelzeman, (501)727-5427.

The Milestone Car Society, P.O. Box 2633, Minneapolis, MN 55402-0633. Don A. Peterson, (314)344-8520.

Motor Bus Society, P.O. Box 251, Paramus, NJ 07653.

Motor Transport Museum, 341 W. Broadway #282, San Diego, CA 92101. Edward Dilginis, (619)233-9707.

National Convertible Association & Registry, 1314 Rollins Rd., Burlingame, CA 94010. Joyce Barrow, (415)348-8269.

National Muscle Car Assoc., 3404 Democrat Rd., Memphis, TN 38118. (901)365-3779; fax (901)366-1807; http://www.goracing.com/

National Woodie Club, P.O. Box 6134, Lincoln, NE 68506. John Lee, (402)488-0990.

"One Off" Car Club, 2360 Fish Creek Place Ste. A, Danville, CA 94506. James E. Ashworth III, (510)838-7788.

Pedal Pumpers Club of America, P.O. Box 430, Needham Heights, MA 02194. Barry Mayer, (617)422-1733.

Society of Automotive Historians, 1102 Long Cove Rd., Gales Ferry, CT 06335-1812.

Steam Automobile Club of America, 1227 W. Voorhees St., Danville, IL 61832.

The Veteran Motor Car Club Of America, P.O. Box 360788, Strongsville, OH 44136. William Donze, (216)238-2771.

SINGLE MARQUE

AUBURN-CORD-DUESENBERG

Auburn-Cord-Duesenberg Club, Rt. 1, Box 340I, Cooper Rd. Pebble Beach, Killen, AL 35645. Jim Corbin, Silvia Corbin, (847)464-5767.

AMC

AMC Pacer Club, 2628 Ashton Rd., Cleveland Heights, OH 44118.

AMC Rambler Club, 2645 Ashton Rd., Cleveland Heights, OH 44118. (216) 371-5946.

American Motors Owners Assoc., 6756 Cornell St., Portage, MI 49002. Darryl Salisbury, (616)323-0369.

AMC World Clubs, Inc., 7963 Depew St., Arvada, CO 80003. Larry G. Mitchell, (303)428-8760.

AMC World Clubs, Inc. – American Motorsport, Int., 7963 DePew St., Arvada, CO 80003. Larry G. Mitchel, (303)428-8760; fax (303)428-1070.

AMC World Clubs, Inc. – The Classic AMX Club, International, 7963 DePew St., Arvada, CO 80003. Larry G. Mitchell, (303)428-8760; fax (303)428-1070.

National American Motors Drivers & Racers Association (NAMDRA), P.O. Box 987, Twin Lakes, WI 53181-0987. Jock Jocewicz, (414)396-9552.

AVANTI

Avanti Owners Assoc. International, P.O. Box 28788, Dallas, TX 75228-0788.

BRICKLIN

Bricklin International Owners Club, 33633 N. Trade Post Rd., Acton, CA 93510. John W. Martin, (805)269-5234.

BRUSH

Brush Owners Association, 1222 N. 168th St., Omaha, NE 68118. Don Ohnstad, (402)289-3913; dohnstad@aol.com

BUICK

Buick Cub of America, P.O. Box 401927, Hesperia, CA 92340-1927. Valerie Ingram, (619)947-2485; fax (619)947-2465.

Buick Club of America – Reatta Division, c/o Bob Peterson, 17 Dundee Court, Mahwah, NJ 07430-1509. John Forrette, j.forrette@genie.geis.com; Bob Peterson, (201)529-2556.

Compact Buick Club, P.O. Box 411, Tustin, CA 92681. Bruce Andren, (714)544-2640.

1937-'38 Buick Club, 1005 Rilma Ln., Los Altos, CA 94022. Harry Logan, (415)941-4587.

'53-'54 Buick Skylark Club, P.O. Box 57, Eagle Bay, NY 13331. Cindy Beckley, (315)357-2218.

Riviera Owners Assoc., P.O. Box 26344, Lakewood, CO 80226. Ray Knott, (303)987-3712.

CADILLAC

Allanté Appreciation Group, 2558 Ingram Rd., Duluth, GA 30136. Victor Yingst, (770)662-5178.

Cadillac Drivers Club, 5825 Vista Ave., Sacramento, CA 95824-1428. Wray Tibbs, (916)421-3193.

Cadillac-LaSalle Club, Inc., P.O. Box 359, Devon, PA 19333. Jay Ann Edmunds (610)688-7747; fax (610)688-0482.

1958 Cadillac Owners Assoc., P.O. Box 850029, Braintree, MA 02185. Dave Becker, (617)843-4485.

CASE

J.I. Case Heritage Foundation, Office of Secretary, P.O. Box 8429, Fort Wayne, IN 46898-8429.

CHALMERS

Chalmers Automobile Registry, 110 Sourwood Dr., Hatboro, PA 19040. D.C. Hammond.

CHANDLER-CLEVELAND

Chandler-Cleveland Motor Club, 43 Wide Beach Rd., Irving, NY 14081. Fred Hansen, (716)549-0729.

CHECKER

Checker Car Club of America, 15536 Sky Hawk Dr., Sun City West, AZ 85375-6512. Steven D. Wilson, (602)546-9052.

CHEVROLET

Bow Tie Chevy Assoc., P.O. Box 608108, Orlando, FL 32860. Denny Williams, (407)880-1956.

Classic Chevy International, P.O. Box 607188, Orlando, FL 32860-7188. (800)456-1957.

Chevrolet Nomad Assoc., 8653 W. Hwy. 2, Cairo, NE 68824, Bob Maline, (402)393-7281.

Early Haulers Truck Club, 8918 Menard, Morton Grove, IL 60053. Vic Lombardo, (847)966-0741. *(Chevy, GMC trucks)*

International Camaro Club, Inc., 2001 Pittston Ave., Scranton, PA 18505. (717)585-4082.

Late Great Chevys, P.O. Box 607824, Orlando, FL 32860.

National Impala Assoc., P.O. Box 968, Spearfish, SD 57783. Dennis L. Naasz, (605)642-5864.

National Nostalgic Nova, P.O. Box 2344, York, PA 17405. (717)252-3867.

The '65-'66 Full Size Chevy Club, 15615 State Rd. 23, Granger, IN 46530. Harold Foos, (219)272-6964.

U.S. Camaro Club, P.O. Box 608167, Orlando, FL 32860. (407)880-1967.

Vintage Chevrolet Club of America, P.O. Box 5387, Orange, CA 92613-5387.

CORVAIR

Corvair Society of America, P.O. Box 607, Lemont, IL 60439-0607. Harry Jensen, (708)257-6530.

Corvair Society of America – Corvanatics. P.O. Box 68, McCordsville, IN 46055. Tom Silvey, (317)335-3772. *(Forward-control vans, trucks)*

Corvair Society of America – Group Ultra Van, 5537 Pioneer Rd., Boulder, CO 80301. W. Christy Barden, (303)530-1288.

Corvair Society of America – Yenko Stinger Corvair Owners, 46 Castle Ave., Jackson, NJ 08527-2513. Charlie Doerge, (908)928-2864.

Corvair Society of America – V-8 Registry, 4361 St. Dominic Dr., Cincinnati, OH 45238. Russ Brandenburg, (513)921-1782.

CORVETTE

Corvette Club of America, P.O. Box 9879, Bowling Green, KY 42102. (502)737-6022; (800)801-7329.

Corvettes Limited, Inc. 11 Liberty Ridge Trail, Totowa, NJ 07512-1620. Jules Borri.

National Corvette Owners Assoc., P.O. Box 777A, Falls Church, VA 22046. Mary Showalter, (703)533-7222.

National Corvette Restorers Society, 6291 Day Rd., Cincinnati, OH 45252-1334.

National Council of Corvette Clubs, P.O. Box 5032, Lafayette, IN 47903-5032.

Solid Axle Corvette Club, P.O. Box 2288, North Highlands, CA 95660. Lucy Badenhoop.

CHRYSLER

Airflow Club of America, 1000 E. Tallmadge Ave., Akron, OH 44310. David Askey, (330)633-6373.

Chrysler Maserati TC Registry, P.O. Box 66813, Chicago, IL 60666-0813. Joseph M. Litza.

Chrysler 300 Club, Inc., Box 570309, Miami, FL 33257-0309. Chuck Angel, (800)416-3443.; fax (305)253-5978.

Chrysler 300 Club International, Inc., 4900 Jonesville Rd., Jonesville, MI 49250. Eleanor Riehl, (517)849-2783; fax (517)849-7445.

Chrysler Town and Country Owners Registry, 4910 E. Bermuda, Tucson, AZ 85712-2020. Peter Gariepy, (602)881-8101.

Mopar Muscle Club International, 879 Summerlea Ave., Washington, PA 15301. Earl Hatfield, Jr., (412)225-5790.

National Chrysler Products Club, 14 Princeton Dr., New Providence, NJ 07974. R.A. Henderson, (908)665-2272.

TC America, Inc., 7200 Montgomery NE #400, Albuquerque, NM 87109. B. Karleen Tarola, (505)299-1747.

WPC Club Inc., P.O. Box 3504, Kalamazoo, MI 49003-3504. Richard Bowman (616)375-5535.

CROSLEY

Crosley Automobile Club, 217 N. Gilbert, Iowa City, IA 52245. Jim Friday, (319)338-9132.

DELOREAN

DeLorean Owners Assoc., 879 Randolph Rd., Santa Barbara, CA 93111. J. F. Truscott, (805)964-5296.

DESOTO

National DeSoto Club, Inc., 1521 Van Cleave Rd. N.W., Albuquerque, NM 87107. William Fisher, (513)429-2361.

DEVIN

Devin Fan Club, 2360 Fish Creek Place, Danville, CA 94506. James E. Ashworth, III, (510)838-7788.

DOBLE

Doble Associates, P.O. Box 588, Culver City, CA 90230. S. Lucas (310)595-6721.

DODGE

Dodge Brothers Club, Inc., P.O. Box 151, North Salem, NY 10560. Mike Wenis, (914)669-5509.

Turbo Diesel Register, 2485 Summeroak Dr., Tucker, GA 30084. (770)938-0711. *(Dodge Cummins Turbo Diesel pickups)*

Viper Club of America, 31690 W. 12 Mile Rd., Farmington Hills, MI 48334. John Thompson, (800)998-1110.

DORT

Dort Motor Club, P.O. Box 174, Hines, IL 60141. Dr. R. Von Bluhme.

DUAL GHIA

Dual Ghia Motor Cars, 29 Forgedale Rd., Fleetwood, PA 19522. Paul Sable, (610)987-6923.

DURANT

Durant Family Registry, 2700 Timber Ln., Green Bay, WI 54313-5899. Jeff Gillis, (414)499-8797, eve.

EDSEL

Edsel Owners Club, Inc., 4713 Queal Dr., Shawnee, KS 66203.

International Edsel Club, P.O. Box 371, Sully, IA 50251.

ESHELMAN

Eshelman Registry, 50 Oakwood Dr., Ringwood, NJ 07456. Bill Hossfield, (201)839-9053.

FORD

Crown Victoria Assoc., P.O. Box 6, Bryan, OH 43506. Toby Gorny, (419)636-2475.

Early Ford V8 Club of America, P.O. Box 2122, San Leandro, CA 94577. Jerry Windle, (619)283-1938; fordv8club@aol.com; v8times@aol.com

Early Ford V8 Foundation, P.O. Box 2222, Livermore, CA 94551-2222. Jerry Windle, (619)283-1938; efv8fndtn@aol.com

Falcon Club of America, Box 113, Jacksonville, AR 72078. Ruby Throgmorton, (501)982-9721.

'54 Ford Club of America, 1517 N. Wilmot #144, Tucson, AZ 85712.

'49-'50-'51 Ford Mercury Owners, P.O. Box 30647, Midwest City, OK 73140-3647. Mike McCarville, (405)737-6021.

The Ranchero Club, 1339 Beverly Rd., Port Vue, PA 15133. Gene Makrancy, (412)678-2470; mollyb@aol.com

Ranchero-Torino Club, 8037 E. Tulip Tree St., Tucson, AZ 85730-4621. Jerry Modene, (520)886-6420.

'68 Pace Car Registry, 8032 E. Haynes, Tucson, AZ 85710-4213. Bill Keller, (520)886-8004.

MODEL A

Model A Ford Cabriolet Club, P.O. Box 515, Porter, TX 77365. Larry Machacek, (713)429-2505.

Model A Ford Club of America (MAFCA), 250 S. Cypress, La Habra, CA 90631-5586. (310)697-2712.

Model A Restorers Club (MARC), 24800 Michigan Ave., Dearborn, MI 48124-1713. (313)278-1455.

Town Sedan Club, 9325 - 31st Ave. N., New Hope, MN 55427. Werner Langenbach, (612)544-0097.

MODEL T

Mercury Body Register, Box 2245, Alderwood Manor, WA 98036. Jarvis, (206) 776-2804. *(Aftermarket speedster body for Ford Model Ts; made in Louisville, Ky., 1921-'26).*

Model T Ford Club International, P.O. Box 438315, Chicago, IL 60643-8315. Howard Gustavson, (312)233-2989.

Model T Ford Club of America, P.O. Box 743936, Dallas, TX 75374-3936. (214)783-7531.

MUSTANG

Mustang Owners Club International, 2720 Tennessee NE, Albuquerque, NM 87110. Paul G. McLaughlin, (505)296-2554.

THUNDERBIRD

Classic Thunderbird Club International, 11823 E. Slauson Ave., Unit #39, P.O. Box 4148, Santa Fe Springs, CA 90670-1148. Margie Price, (310)945-6836.

Heartland Vintage Thunderbird Club of America, P.O. Box 18113, Kansas City, MO 64133. Don Kimrey (816)313-6151.

International Thunderbird Club, 8 Stag Trail, Fairfield, NJ 07004. Kenneth Leaman.

Vintage Thunderbird Club International, P.O. Box 2250, Dearborn, MI 48123-2250. Bob Gadra, (716)674-7251.

FRANKLIN

The H.H. Franklin Club, Inc., Cazenovia College, Cazenovia, NY 13035. Chuck Johnson, (703)768-8437; lyndamj@aol.com; home page, http://krell.cc.sunybroome.edu/franklin.

HUDSON-ESSEX-TERRAPLANE

Hudson Essex Terraplane Club, Inc., 100 E. Cross St., Ypsilanti, MI 48198. (313)482-5200.

HUPMOBILE

Hupmobile Club Inc., 158 Pond Rd., N. Franklin, CT 06254. (860)642-6697.

INTERNATIONAL HARVESTER

IH Collectors, 684 N. Northwest Hwy., Box 250, Park Ridge, IL 60068.

Scout & International Truck Assoc., P.O. Box 12, Ogden, IL 61859. Mrs. Dee Buchanan.

United Scouts & Assoc. (USA), 3369 Sugar Pike Rd., Canton, GA 30115. William Reece, (770)751-0562.

JEEP

The Jeep Registry, 172 Long Hill Rd., Oakland, NJ 07436-3113. (201)405-0480.

KAISER-FRAZER

Kaiser-Frazer Owners Club International, P.O. Box 1014, Stroudsburg, PA 18360.

Kaiser-Frazer Owners Club International – Kaiser-Darrin Owners Roster, Rd. #3, Box #36, Antram Rd., Somerset, PA 15501-8814. Dave Antram, (814)445-6135.

KING MIDGET

International King Midget Car Club, P.O. Box 549, Westport, IN 47283. Kathy Kinsey, (513)698-5144.

King Midget Ohio, 2196 Sunray Circle, Alliance, OH 44601. Tim Gross, (216)823-1773.

LINCOLN

Colorado Continental Convertible Club, 385 S. Olive Way, Denver, CO 80224-1354. Floyd B. Engleman, (303)322-2674.

The Continental Mark II Owners Association (CMOA), 26676 Holiday Ranch Airport, Apple Valley, CA 92307. Buddy E. Holiday, (619)247-4758.

Lincoln & Continental Owners Club, 465 NE 181st Ave., Ste. 222, Portland, OR 97230. Becky D'Ambrosia, (503)658-3119.

Lincoln Owners' Club, P.O. Box 1434, Minocqua, WI 54548. Jim Griffin, (715)356-3039.

Lincoln-Zephyr Owners Club, P.O. Box 16-5835, Miami, FL 33116. John Murphy, (305)274-3624.

Road Race Lincoln Register, 461 Woodland Dr., Wisconsin Rapids, WI 54494-6555. Burr A. Oxley, (715)423-9579.

MARMON

Marmon Club, Arthur Fawcett, Jr., 4171 Garden Ln., El Sobrante, CA 94803. (510)222-6917.

MAXWELL-BRISCOE

The Maxwell-Briscoe Registry, 55 E. Golden Lake Rd., Circle Pines, MN 55014. Jim Moe, (612)786-6609, fax (612)786-2752.

MERCURY

Big M Mercury Club, 5 Robinson Rd., W. Woburn, MA 01801. George Stringos.

Cougar Club of America, 5810 142nd Place SE, Bellevue, WA 98006. Randy Goodling, (717)367-6700. Jim Pinkerton, (206)641-9037.

International Mercury Owners Assoc. (IMOA), 6445 W. Grand Ave., Chicago, IL 60635-3410. Jerry Robbin, (312)622-6445; fax (312)622-3602.

New England Comet Club, 33 Sanderson Rd., Waltham, MA 02154. Bob Boudrot, (617)891-6097.

'70/'71 Cyclone-Montego Registry, 19 Glyn Dr., Newark, DE 19713-4016. Robert Day, (302)737-4252.

METROPOLITAN

Metropolitan Owners Club of North America, 5009 Barton Rd., Madison, WI 53711. Larry Hurley, (608)271-0457; fax, (608)833-2058.

MUNTZ

Muntz-Kurtis Car Club, Box 12, 1719 Grove St., Glenview, IL 60025. C. Domm.

Muntz Registry, 21303 NE 151st, Woodinville, WA 98072-7612. Victor Munsen, (206)788-6587

NASH

Nash Car Club of America, Box 80279 Dept. OC, Indianapolis, IN 46280.

OLDSMOBILE

Curved Dash Oldsmobile Club, 3455 Florida Ave. N., Minneapolis, MN 55427. Gary Hoonsbeen, (612)533-4280; fax (612)535-1421.

National Antique Oldsmobile Club, 11730 Moffit Ln., Manassas, VA 22111-3122.

Oldsmobile Club of America, Inc., P.O. Box 80318, Lansing, MI 48908.

Oldsmobile Club of America – Hurst/Olds Club of America, 455 131st Ave., Wayland, MI 49348. Sue Skiba.

PACKARD

The Packard Club (Packard Automobile Classics, Inc.), 420 S. Ludlow St., Dayton, OH 45402. Membership, (800)527-3452.

Packards International Car Club, 302 French St., Santa Ana, CA 92701. Carol Mauck, (714)541-8431.

PIERCE-ARROW

Pierce-Arrow Society, Bernard J. Weis, 135 Edgerton St., Rochester, NY 14607.

PLYMOUTH

Plymouth Owners Club Inc., P.O. Box 416, Cavalier, ND 58220. (701)549-3746.

PONTIAC

Bandit Trans Am Club, P.O. Box 322, Cleveland, WI 53015. Crawford Smith, (414)693-8355.

GTO Assoc. of America, 5829 Stroebel Rd., Saginaw, MI 48609. (800)GTO-1964.

Pontiac-Oakland Club International, P.O. Box 9569, Bradenton, FL 34206. (941)750-9234.

Pontiac Oakland Club International – Grand Prix Chapter, 357 Marvin Place, Wheeling, IL 60090. Mike Schaudel, (847)537-0345.

The Judge GTO International, 114 Prince George Dr., Hampton, VA 23669. Robert J. McKenzie, (804)838-2059.

National Firebird Club, P.O. Box 11238, Chicago, IL 60611, (312)769-6262; e-mail, firebirdclub@prodigy.com; Internet, http://www.classicar.com/clubs/natfireb/natbireb.htm.

Oakland-Pontiac Enthusiast Organization, 3520 Warringham Dr., Waterford, MI 48329-1380. Daniel L. Hosler, (810)623-7573, fax (810)623-6180.

'69-'71 GTO "The Judge" Convertible Club, 1250 Briar St., Wayzata, MN 55391. Paul Bergstrom, (612)449-8811.

REO

Reo Club of America, 7971 Vernon Rd., Cicero, NY 13039. Jack Perkis, (315)458-4721.

SABRA

Sabra Connection, 7040 N. Navajo Ave., Milwaukee WI 53217. Herb Smith, (414)352-8408.

SALEEN

Saleen Owners and Enthusiasts Club, P.O. Box 1022, Canton, NC 28716. Debbie Blaylock, (704)648-2877.

Team Saleen, 9 Whatney, Irvine, CA 92718. (714)597-4911.

SHELBY

Shelby Dodge Automobile Club, P.O. Box 4631, Lutherville, MD 21094-4631. John Johnson, (410)389-1530.

Shelby Owners of America, Inc., P.O. Drawer 1429, Great Bend, KS 67530. Brock R. McPherson, (316)793-3420.

STEPHENS

Stephens Owners Registry, 1034 N. Henderson, Freeport, IL 61032. Dick Farnsworth, (815)232-3825.

STEVENS-DURYEA

Stevens-Duryea Associates, 3565 Newhaven Rd., Pasadena, CA 91107, (818)351-8237.

STUDEBAKER

Antique Studebaker Club Inc. P.O. Box 28845, Dallas, TX 75228-0845. (800)527-3452.

1956 Studebaker Golden Hawk Owners Register, 1025 Nodding Pines Way, Casselberry, FL 32707. Frank Ambrogio.

Studebaker Drivers Club, Inc., P.O. Box 28788, Dallas, TX 75228-0788, (800)527-3452, fax (214)296-7920.

Studebaker Drivers Club –'53-'54 Studebaker C/K Owners, 3540 Middlefield Rd., Menlo Park, CA 94025-3025. Dennis Hommel, (415)365-4565; fax (415)365-0487.

STUTZ

The Stutz Club, 7400 Lantern Rd., Indianapolis, IN 46256. Dale K. Wells, (616)375-4844. *(Stutz, Blackhawk cars, H.C.S. cars and taxis, Stutz firetrucks, Pak-Age-Cars)*

SURREY

Surrey Registry, P.O. Box 98019, Las Vegas, NV 89193-8019. William Borton, (702)433-7857. *(Curved Dash Olds replica, made by E.W. Bliss Co., Ohio, 1958-'60)*

TUCKER

Tucker Automobile Club of America, Inc., 9509 Hinton Dr., Santee, CA 92071-2760. William E. Pommering, (619)562-9644.

Tucker 1052 Convertible Club, 526 Ryan Ct., West Dundee, IL 60118. George Esch, (708)836-8828.

WILLYS

Mid-America Willys Club, 18819 Valley Dr., Minnetonka, MN 55345.

Willys Aero Survival Count, 952 Ashbury Heights Court, Decatur, GA 30030-4177. Rick Kamen, (404)288-8222; kamenra@aol.com

The Willys Club, 795 N. Evans St., Pottstown, PA 19464. Gordon Lindahl, (610)326-2907; gowillys@ix.netcom.com

Willys Overland Jeepster Club, 453 Girard Ave., East Aurora, NY 14052. Richard "Dick" Depke, (716)652-8962.

Willys-Overland-Knight Registry, Inc., 1440 Woodacre Dr., McLean, VA 22101-2535. Duane Perrin, (703)533-0396.

Index